THE
CENTRIST
MANIFESTO

THE
CENTRIST
MANIFESTO

CHARLES WHEELAN

W. W. Norton & Company

New York • *London*

For information about permission to reproduce selections from this book,
write to Permissions, W. W. Norton & Company, Inc.,
500 Fifth Avenue, New York, NY 10110

For information about special discounts for bulk purchases, please contact
W. W. Norton Special Sales at specialsales@wwnorton.com or 800-233-4830

Manufacturing by Courier Westford
Production manager: Julia Druskin

ISBN 978-0-393-34687-9 (pbk.)

W. W. Norton & Company, Inc.
500 Fifth Avenue, New York, N.Y. 10110
www.wwnorton.com

W. W. Norton & Company Ltd.
Castle House, 75/76 Wells Street, London W1T 3QT

1 2 3 4 5 6 7 8 9 0

FOR SOPHIA

Contents

THE
CENTRIST
MANIFESTO

CHAPTER 1

The Big Idea

SOMETHING has to change.

Our country is on a dangerous trajectory. We are
mired in serious policy challenges, in large part because
the political process has moved beyond gridlock to complete paralysis.

Why are we paralyzed? Because our two political parties are increasingly dominated by their most vocal and
extreme members, leaving little room for compromise.
This would be a problem in any place at any time, but it
is particularly frustrating in the United States right now
because *most American voters are not that extreme.* The
largest and fastest-growing bloc of American voters are
"independent." These are people without a party. Many
were among the 41 percent of voters who described
themselves as "moderate" in exit polls during the 2012

presidential election.[1] Most important, these are American voters who would agree to sensible compromises on most issues of the day.

I am not suggesting that our most serious national challenges have simple and attractive solutions. They do not. But every major issue facing the United States can be reasonably confronted the way the rest of us approach challenges everywhere else in life: Identify the problem. Assess the causes. Evaluate the possible solutions. Recognize the legitimate differences of opinion. And then do something responsible. Our dysfunctional two-party system has lost its ability to do that.

The answer is the Centrist Party—a third political party that empowers the middle. The sane, pragmatic majority in America must wrestle the steering wheel of the country away from the extremists on either side. This book is a plan for making it happen.

The purpose of the Centrist Party is not to make noise, like Ralph Nader and Pat Buchanan did when they ran for president. Nor is it a means for angry people to vent in a semi-organized way, like the Tea Party, which has no major policy accomplishments to speak of and has mostly served to fracture the Republican Party. (*New York Times* columnist Tom Friedman has called it the "Tea Kettle" movement because it is mostly about letting off steam.)[2] The Centrist Party will have a coherent ideology that draws from the best of both traditional political parties.

The Centrist electoral strategy revolves around the U.S. Senate. The party will focus on winning a handful of U.S. Senate seats in states where moderate candidates traditionally do well. With a mere four or five U.S. Senate seats, the Centrists can deny either traditional party a majority. At that point, the Centrists would be America's power brokers. *Nothing could happen without those swing votes.* And when those swing votes represent sensible, moderate voters— rather than the non-compromising extremists of the Left and Right—good things can start happening again.

The Centrist Party will organize the vast American middle into a political movement built around sensible governance. It is more feasible than you might think.

The Challenges

If the Republicans and the Democrats were professional sports teams with disappointing records this season, we could simply stop paying attention and hope for better things next year. We do not have that luxury with governance. Anyone who reads a newspaper has a pretty good idea that things are moving in the wrong direction; here is a quick tour.

The economy is stagnant, with little promise of a rapid recovery. Millions are out of work, including a high proportion of recent college graduates carrying heavy debt loads. The mortgage meltdown and the subsequent financial crisis suggest that our complex economy needs more adult supervision.

America's major entitlement programs—Social Security, Medicare, and Medicaid—are unsustainably expensive. The longer we go without addressing the problem, the more dangerously indebted the nation will become. The only way to preserve America's important safety net is to fix it.

Our health-care system is inefficient and expensive— with or without Obamacare. We spend significantly more on medical care than all other developing countries, but we get significantly less in terms of good health. Life expectancy in the United States is lower than the average for all other developed countries—and the gap is growing, not shrinking.[3]

Our infrastructure is crumbling. The American Society of Civil Engineers has estimated that the United States needs to spend two trillion dollars just to fix the roads, bridges, and rail lines we have—let alone expand things that will be necessary to support the world's most vibrant economy over the next century, such as airport capacity and high-speed rail.[4] As the British news magazine *The Economist* noted recently in a report on America's transport infrastructure, "America, despite its wealth and strength, often seems to be falling apart."[5]

We have done nothing to address climate change, other than cling to the delusional hope that it is not happening. This lack of action is particularly disturbing because there are ample other reasons besides global warming to wean us from our excessive dependence on fossil fuels. In fact, the climate change "debate" is a sad example of the triumph of a self-interested, faith-based argument over common sense and the scientific method.

Our "human capital"—the reservoir of skills that we need to prosper in a modern economy—is stagnant. The U.S. high school dropout rate is about the same as it was thirty years ago, despite the fact that dropping out of high school is essentially an economic death warrant in the twenty-first-century economy. The United States has always had far more college graduates than the rest of the world, going all the way back to 1862, when Abraham Lincoln and Congress set aside federal land to create the land grant universities. These are institutions like Rutgers, Penn State, Ohio State, the University of Illinois, Purdue, Kansas State, the University of Nebraska, and the University of California, among many others. By 2010, the United States had fallen from first in the world in the percentage of college graduates to twelfth.[6]

America's poverty rate is higher than it was in 1975. When it comes to infant mortality, the United States has the *highest* rate among the thirty-three advanced economies, according to the International Monetary Fund.[7] Leave aside the mind-numbing statistics for a moment and just think about what that means. The richest society in the history of human civilization is failing at one of the most basic tasks in life: delivering healthy babies.

The United States currently spends more on defense than the countries with the next thirteen highest defense budgets *combined*.[8] Yet we have done nothing in recent years to update and strengthen the international institutions that promote global peace, prosperity, and cooperation—despite the fact that many serious policy issues, from promoting trade to fighting terrorists and drug cartels, tend to be international in nature.

And we are not paying our bills. We have steadily accumulated debts to the rest of the world while making unrealistic promises to ourselves in the form of Social Security and Medicare. Both political parties talk a good game around fiscal discipline at the same time they are making the problem worse with unfunded tax cuts, new spending, or both. The growing debt is unfair to future generations and dangerously destabilizing to the financial system (which is not particularly stable to begin with).

More broadly, the American public has developed a remarkable inability to defer gratification. We seem unable or unwilling to make the short-term sacrifices necessary to build a more prosperous society; the political system panders to that shortsighted view. This is a country that was built on huge public and private investments that paid dividends, decade after decade, generation after generation: the land grant universities, the interstate highway system, the transcontinental railroad.

There is a set of famous research studies from the 1960s and 1970s in which young children were placed in a room alone. On a table in front of them was a desirable treat or toy, such as a marshmallow. Each child could eat the treat or take the toy at any point; however, the children were also told that if they avoided eating the tantalizing treat for a short period, then they would get two treats once the time elapsed. In other words, there was a big payoff for deferring gratification. Some kids could do it; others could not.

What's remarkable is how predictive that behavior turned out to be of success later in life. The kids who did not rush to eat the marshmallow turned out to have higher SAT scores, better grades, less criminal activity, and many other positive life outcomes, even decades later.[9]

The United States is currently a country that not only gobbles down its marshmallows but also borrows extra marshmallows from China and eats them too. Look at our long-term "marshmallow" indicators: low household savings; mounting foreign debts; flat educational attainment; crumbling infrastructure; an incapacity to balance our government accounts with either higher taxes or less spending; an unwillingness to make even modest economic sacrifices to combat climate change.

WE KNOW AMERICA can do better. I recently watched the Ken Burns documentary on World War II with my eight-year-old son. I was awed by the commitment of the soldiers who rushed the beaches at Normandy with full knowledge that they might not get ashore alive. In the Pacific, the survivors of each campaign would just move on to the next island. And on the home front, the country rationed goods and bought war bonds—all as part of a collective sacrifice to make the world better. The United States accrued enormous debts to win the war but then worked aggressively to restore the nation's fiscal health over the ensuing decade.

I kept thinking as I watched, Could there be any greater contrast than with the Iraq and Afghanistan engagements, for which the United States tapped volunteer soldiers to fight while it passed out tax cuts paid for with borrowed money? This is the opposite of how our country handled World War II; most of us aren't even paying for our current wars, let alone putting ourselves at risk to fight in them. This situation seems symptomatic of our entire approach to public life right now.

Americans have a sense that something is broken with
the whole political apparatus. A 2011 poll by *Politico* found
that 73 percent of Americans feel the country is headed in
the wrong direction.[10] A 2012 Rasmussen poll found that
just 14 percent of adults expect today's children to be better
off than their parents.[11]

How is the electoral process dealing with this? Let me
ask you: After the 2012 elections—when our candidates
and assorted other groups spent six billion dollars, ostensibly to inform us about the important issues of the day—did
you feel better or worse about our future?[12]

Our Two Broken Parties

The solution to these challenges is not simply to "throw
the bums out" or to "start running government like a business." These are meaningless phrases that demonstrate a
lack of understanding of the challenges of communal
governance. The solution is to empower different kinds of
political leaders who represent more moderate and ideologically coherent views. The major parties have outlived
their usefulness. Larry Diamond, a political science pro-
fessor at Stanford University, summed it up well in 2010:
"We basically have two bankrupt parties bankrupting the
country."[13]

The Republican Party has allowed its healthy skepticism
of government to evolve into a hardened, oversimplified
view that government is always bad and lower taxes are
always good. The party has talked tough on spending while
doing a tremendous amount of it. For all the debate on fis-

cal responsibility, the Republicans are no better at balancing the federal budget than the Democrats are.

The Republicans are in denial about climate change, which is particularly unfortunate because the party could play a constructive role in finding cost-effective and business-friendly environmental solutions. The party is at war with itself regarding the relationship between the individual and the state. The supposed party of small government is only too eager to intervene in personal reproductive decisions and private morality. Passing a law (or a constitutional amendment) to prevent two people of the same sex from getting married is not limited government.

Meanwhile, the Democrats are entirely unrealistic (at least in public) about the looming cost of America's entitlement programs. Paradoxically, the party is putting important fixtures of the social safety net at risk by refusing to support the kinds of modifications that would make these programs fiscally viable in the long run (such as raising the retirement age for Social Security).

The Democrats are far too optimistic about what government can accomplish, meaning that good intentions often lead to lousy programs and regulations. Perhaps most important, the self-described party of the middle class needs to show far more respect for the forces that create wealth for that middle class, such as international trade. The Democratic Party is abusive of the people who earn profits and grow businesses, as if they were the enemy of the working class rather than the ones who sign their paychecks.

Instead of softening the rough edges of markets and globalization, a necessary role that most Americans would thoroughly embrace, the Democrats too often stand in the way of economic progress. Democratic candidates have become beholden to interest groups with positions that are inimical to the supposed core values of the party. One cannot support the current demands of America's teachers' unions while simultaneously claiming to stand for poor and minority children.

New York Times columnist David Brooks nicely summarized the failure of either political party to come to grips with America's economic reality:

> The Republican growth agenda—tax cuts and nothing else—is stupefyingly boring, fiscally irresponsible and politically impossible. Giant tax cuts—if they were affordable—might boost overall growth, but they would do nothing to address the structural problems that are causing a working class crisis. . . .
>
> As for the Democrats, they offer practically nothing. They acknowledge huge problems like wage stagnation and then offer . . . light rail! Solar panels![14]

The Rising Extremism

Our political institutions reward the most extreme views in each political party. Congress has grown increasingly polarized and dysfunctional because we have built a system that elects extremists. Each party nominates its candidates in a primary. Who votes in primaries? The most extreme elements of each party. In many states, independents are not even allowed to vote in the primaries. The more moderate candidates who might have broad appeal in a general election never get on the ballot.

The U.S. House of Representatives is particularly bad because incumbent politicians can gerrymander the electoral map every ten years, drawing "safe" seats for themselves. We end up with geographically bizarre electoral districts that make little sense other than as a tool for protecting the party that owns the seat. In these "safe" districts, the opposing party has no hope, so the winner is chosen in the primary, not the general election. As a result, a high proportion of members of the House—clearly the fire-breathing chamber in Congress—are selected by the most radical members of their own parties.

All of this feeds on itself. As the two parties move left and right, the moderates either give up or get voted out. Olympia Snowe, the Republican senator from Maine with a reputation for bipartisan compromise, announced in 2012 that she was leaving the Senate after four terms. In an op-ed titled "Why I'm Leaving the Senate," Snowe described "the dysfunction and political polarization in the institution."[15]

At about the same time, Indiana Senator Richard Lugar, whom the *New York Times* described as "a collegial moderate who personified a gentler political era," lost a primary challenge to a candidate backed by the Tea Party.[16]

In the run-up to the 2012 elections, one new analysis noted, "A potent combination of Congressional redistricting, retirements of fed-up lawmakers and campaign spending by special interests is pushing out moderate members of both parties, leaving a shrinking corps of consensus builders." In particular, the Blue Dog Democrats, a group of Centrist Democrats, have been "all but eviscerated from the House over the last few elections." Tennessee's Jim Cooper, one of the few surviving Blue Dogs, lamented, "We moderates are an endangered species, but we are also a necessary ingredient for any problem solving."[17]

The Internet and the twenty-four-hour news cycle add accelerant to the extremism. The partisan news/entertainment outlets are rewarded for attracting a large, loyal audience, not for building consensus around ideas that would move the country forward. (As a thought exercise, imagine the 1787 Constitutional Convention trying to function in the era of Fox News, MSNBC, and rabid Internet bloggers.)

Not surprisingly, fewer and fewer voters feel entirely comfortable as either a Republican or a Democrat. *Wall Street Journal* political columnist (and longtime Washington observer) Alan Murray spoke for many of us when he lamented, "I'm not interested in a Democratic Party that lets labor unions turn it away from free trade, or lets teachers unions block any semblance of education reform, or lets trial lawyers stand in the way of common sense class-action reform. But I'm also not interested in a Republican Party that is pushed by the National Rifle Association to give gun makers extraordinary protection from lawsuits, or is forced by extreme religious groups to ban stem-cell research that could save countless lives, or believes the worthiest recipients of tax relief are the heirs of the wealthy."[18]

More and more voters are describing themselves as independent.[19] But independents define themselves primarily by what they are *not*, namely, Republicans or Democrats. The challenge is organizing this discontent into a meaningful and positive political force. The Centrist Party will introduce a coherent governing philosophy around which Americans disenchanted with the traditional political fare will naturally coalesce.

The Centrist Party

The purpose of the Centrist Party is to do a hard reset on American policy. The Centrist Party will *not* do this by splitting the difference between the Republicans and Democrats on every issue, as if each one were a bowl of warm oatmeal. Instead, the Centrist Party will take the best ideas from each party, discard the nonsense, and build something new and better.

After all, there is a lot to like about the Republicans: a belief in personal responsibility, a respect for markets and the forces of wealth creation, an understanding of the economic costs of taxation and regulation, and a healthy skepticism of what government can and cannot accomplish.

And there is a lot to like about the Democrats: a concern for working people, a commitment to a strong social safety net, an impressive record of social tolerance, a long-standing concern for the environment, and a recognition that government can play a crucial role in protecting us from the most egregious abuses of capitalism.

At their best, the Democrats have their heart in the right place. We ought to build a more inclusive society with a path to prosperity for all citizens, and a safety net for those caught in the crosshairs of free markets and globalization. But we can't be all heart. The Republicans often have a better-functioning brain. They remind us how hard it is to achieve lofty social goals, and that most government efforts to do so involve serious costs or trade-offs.

Taking the best from each party, and discarding the nonsense at the extremes, provides a meaningful path forward. The United States does not need to abandon its neediest citizens in order to balance the books. We do not need to stop investing in things like basic research and transportation infrastructure in order to make the country more productive in the long run. We do not have to forgo a sane environmental policy in order to enjoy significant economic growth.

We do need to curtail social benefits for citizens and corporations who are perfectly capable of getting by on their own. We do need to fix a ridiculously inefficient tax code. We do need to raise taxes on polluting activities, particularly the emission of carbon. We do need to implement institutional changes that will make government more efficient and responsive.

In more normal times, these are the kinds of things that pragmatic Democrats and Republicans would agree to do together. Right now, they are not getting it done. In the words of David Brooks, it is time for "an insurgency of the rational."[20] The American political landscape has evolved before. Like everything else, political parties have a life span. What happened to the Whigs? The Federalists?

Life changes. The country changes. Political parties should change too.

The Strategy

Conventional wisdom suggests that the American political system is hostile to all third parties. That is wrong. *The
system is hostile to third parties emerging from the political
fringe*—the Green Party, for example. These parties do
not win elections because they represent relatively small,
deeply ideological segments of the population. In fact, they
often have a counterproductive effect. Ralph Nader almost
certainly cost Al Gore the election in 2000, the pathetic
irony being that the Green Party he was supposedly rep-
resenting ended up worse off as a result of his campaign.
When these fringe parties appear, potential supporters must
choose between making noise and making a difference.

A Centrist Party is the opposite. The American political
system makes it possible for the Centrists to make noise *and*
to make a difference. *Every Centrist candidate begins in the
political center, which is where most of the votes are.* That
candidate does not compete by being more extreme than
everyone else in the field—left of the Democrats or right
of the Republicans. He or she competes by appealing to
the big fat middle, which is where Republican and Democratic candidates rush to get votes after having pandered to
the extremist elements in their parties during the primary.
In the new scenario, a Centrist candidate will already own
that political real estate.

The place to begin is the U.S. Senate. Forget (at first)
about the House of Representatives or the presidency. The
structure of the Senate is such that a few moderate senators can effectively wield tremendous power. If there were

just four or five Centrist senators, then neither traditional party would have a majority—*and that handful of Centrist senators would hold the swing votes on every issue facing the Senate.*

Many states could easily elect a Centrist to the U.S. Senate. As of the beginning of 2013, twenty-two states have either one Republican senator and one Democratic senator, or a governor from one party and a senator from the other. Another three states have elected independents to one of those offices. What does that tell us?

Voters in all of these states are willing to elect a Democrat or a Republican, with independent voters typically swinging the election one way or the other. A Centrist candidate—by winning most of the independent vote and peeling off moderates from both parties—would likely do better in these states than a traditional Republican or Democratic candidate.

Remember, one quirk of the American electoral system is that the winning candidate need only get the most votes, as little as 34 percent in a three-way race, rather than an outright majority. A Centrist candidate backed by a strong, well-financed national organization could get 34 percent of the vote in a lot of states: California, most of New England, most of the Midwest, Florida, Virginia.

Is all of this ambitious, bordering on naïve? Probably. But for the skeptics, I have some questions of my own:

First, why not? Why must 2014 be different from 1854, when the two existing parties were inadequate to deal with the issues of the day and the Republican Party was born? Why must we be governed by two parties that were conceived before electricity was invented? (Seriously, it should be a red flag when the *youngest* major political party was created to deal with *slavery*.)

Second, if only *10 percent* of Americans approved of the job that Congress was doing in 2012—the lowest approval rating since Gallup began doing polls on the subject—then isn't there room for something better?[21] Would any serious entrepreneur look at a market in which *90 percent of customers say they are displeased* and conclude that there is no room for an improved product? As I will discuss in the next chapter, government is not a business, but we can still aspire to make more than 10 percent of the electorate happy with their government.

Last, and most personal, what are *you* doing to make things better? I was too young to experience the social upheaval of the 1960s (or the free love), but there is one political slogan from that era that seems apt in this context, particularly for those who complain the loudest about our broken system: if you are not part of the solution, then you are part of the problem.

THE UNITED STATES is still the most privileged place on the planet: It is big and fertile. Our population is young relative to the populations in other developed nations. We have an economic system that brilliantly fosters innovation. We have good neighbors and peaceful borders. We have public institutions that work reasonably well. At a time when higher education is more important than ever, we have a near monopoly on the best research institutions in the world.

We have a real democracy. We may not like all of our politicians, but when they get voted out of office, they leave peacefully. Most Americans pay their taxes and abide by the law. We have a culture that is—with notable exceptions—more diverse and tolerant than most places on earth.

What's not to like about that national endowment?

The challenges we have to deal with as a nation are entirely manageable. The key is to mobilize America's inner pragmatism. The Centrist Party is a step in that direction.

CHAPTER 2

Government's
Herculean Task

WHO is your state senator?

When was the last time *you* ran for public office?

What was the last campaign you worked on in a serious way?

Have you ever called your representative in Congress to complain about his or her vote for pork-laden bills?

I will get back to bashing ideologues and politicians in a moment, but first I would like to point out a truism: politicians can pander only to people willing to be pandered to. At the end of the day, we are the ones who elect our government. And that means that we are responsible for what happens in Washington and the state capitals. That is the reality of democracy. It is not entirely unlike the old dog-training aphorism that there are no bad dogs, only bad owners. We "own" this government, and if Congress has been doing the equivalent of peeing on the carpet for a decade, then it is our fault.

Most of us are not paying attention in a serious way. Democracy is not an inherently passive activity, but somehow in the United States it has evolved into one. As a result, we get the government we deserve. Why is public spending out of control? Because we like most government programs; we've come to expect the government to do a lot for us, even as we rail more generally against "big government." Too few of our public discussions flush out the inherent trade-offs: smaller government means the phone will ring longer when you dial 911 (literally and metaphorically).

Why has government borrowing reached a dangerous and irresponsible level? Because we prefer to bump our fiscal obligations into the future rather than pay for them now. What is not to like about getting services now that someone else will have to pay for later?

Even when we are fully engaged in the democratic process—voting, staying informed on issues, running for office—governing is hard. By governing, I mean the process of making communal decisions, which can be frustrating when six people are choosing a restaurant and fabulously difficult when 330 million people are making decisions about war, social policy, taxes, and scores of other issues around which there are reasonable and deep-seated ideological differences of opinion. This is what we ask our elected representatives to do.

Our job as responsible citizens, the Centrist Party aside, is to insert ourselves into an inherently difficult process. The involvement of smart, thoughtful people is no guarantee of good governance, but the absence of those folks makes bad governance inevitable.

Who Is Minding the Store?

I ran for Congress in the winter of 2009, only months after Lehman Brothers went bust. (I ran in a special election for Rahm Emanuel's seat after he was appointed to be Barack Obama's chief of staff.) The economy was in a complete free fall, arguably the worst economic crisis since the Great Depression. No one could credibly claim that the election did not matter.

The sitting governor of Illinois at the time, Rod Blagojevich, had just been indicted for trying to sell the Senate seat Obama had held. The previous governor, George Ryan, was already in prison for selling commercial driver's licenses. No one could look at Illinois and credibly claim that "politics as usual" was working out well.

The special election had roughly twenty-three candidates. (Some of them were kicked off the ballot, so the number varied at different points in the race.) There were about twelve Democrats, five Green Party candidates, and five or six Republicans. The *Chicago Sun-Times* went so far as to commend the overall quality of the field, noting, "The wide-open race to fill the congressional seat left open by Rahm Emanuel, who left to become President Obama's chief of staff, could have attracted a parade of political hacks. Not so, this time. Voters will find a ballot filled with impressive and thoughtful candidates."[22] No one could credibly look at the field and claim that there was not a candidate for them.

The voter turnout for the special election was 20 percent.

In other words, despite the emerging financial crisis, other long-term public concerns such as climate change and health care, the prodigious corruption of the Chicago electoral status quo, and a diverse field of "impressive and thoughtful" candidates, eight out of ten registered voters could not muster the energy to vote. Seriously?

The reality is that most of us are engaged in the political process at the bare margin, if that. We treat state and federal politics like the Chicago Cubs: they are a perennial disappointment, so we figure we'll just ignore them after they collapse in July or August and wait for football season.

This is a perfectly rational response for professional sports; it does not work for politics. If sane, pragmatic, moderate people ignore politics because they are disgusted with the outcomes, then it merely leaves a vacuum to be filled by more extreme and dishonest elements. Unlike baseball, democracy is not a spectator sport. Things won't correct themselves if you ignore them out of disgust. They will get worse. Look around.

The most egregious acts perpetrated by "special interests" can happen only if the rest of us are not paying much attention. Illinois Senator Everett Dirksen once said famously, "I see the light when I feel the heat." Politicians who seek to be reelected (which is not an unreasonable aspiration) respond to pressure and incentives, like we all do. If 2 percent of the population believe that corn subsidies are a good idea, and 98 percent believe that they are a poor use of government funds, what is a representative to do?

That's easy. Vote for the corn subsidies. Why? Because the 2 percent care passionately about the government handout (and will aggressively support the politicians who facilitate it), while the 98 percent who pay for those subsidies are not paying attention or do not care enough to do anything about it. (Just to clarify, bitching to a like-minded friend at a cocktail party about the idiocy of corn subsidies does not constitute doing anything about anything.)

Have you ever *not* voted for someone whom you otherwise liked because he or she supported farm subsidies? Well, farmers in Illinois or Iowa or Nebraska *will* oppose a candidate who does not support these payments.

True, the choices among candidates are often awful, and our mainstream political parties are ossified and outdated. We can do better; that's why you are reading this book. But first, let's think in a more disciplined way about why our political outcomes seem so perennially disappointing.

Making Public Policy Is Hard

Assume that some twist of fate has made you president of your homeowners' association. Your primary responsibility is planning the annual block party, which involves arranging for a catered meal and a film that will be projected on a screen outdoors in a common area. The whole event will be paid for out of the annual budget, which comes from mandatory dues. The majority of your neighbors are genial, reasonable people, but there are a handful of folks apt to complain vociferously when they do not get exactly what they want, even when most other homeowners want something entirely different.

You can watch only one film at the block party—because

there is just one outdoor screen and the movie is meant
to be a communal experience. This is the first test of your
leadership. The families with children are pushing for a
Disney movie to keep their kids occupied during the party;
the families without kids do not want to be subjected to a
film about princesses or talking donkeys. The weird guy
at the end of the street has generously offered to share his
"world class adult movie collection."

You sensibly opt against a porn film, as well as an ano-
dyne children's movie, and select a PG-13 adventure flick
with decent appeal across the age spectrum (but arguably
inappropriate for the youngest of the kids).

On the food front, your dinner committee has chosen
grilled chicken, burgers, and hot dogs, and a pasta dish as a
vegetarian option, though the two vegetarian families are
still peeved that their annual dues are being used to support
a banquet built primarily around grilling animal flesh.

Meanwhile, a sizeable minority of residents do not think
you should have had the party at all. Yes, 70 percent of
the homeowners voted to allocate the funds for the party at
your last meeting, so you are delivering what most people
want, but that still means 30 percent prefer not to spend
money this way. And within the majority who supported
the party, a minority was pushing for a lobster bake with a
live swing band and ice sculptures.

In the end you will have one outdoor film, one meal, and
one budget. Even if you offer superb leadership, adhere to
the will of the majority, and make defensible decisions at
every step in the process, the only possible outcome is that
many people will be watching a film they don't want to see,

eating food they would not have chosen, and paying for a party they did not want in the first place.

And if you had opted not to have the party, a different and larger group of "constituents" would have been inflamed. That's public policy.

I use this example when I am speaking in public, and the "That's public policy" line always gets a laugh. But the homeowners' block party, albeit somewhat silly, *is* public policy in the sense that it represents a set of shared decisions that are binding on the entire group, even those who vehemently disagree with the decisions. When there is only one possible shared course of action, we somehow have to come to agreement on what that course of action is going to be.

Most communal policy decisions are a heck of a lot more difficult to reach than choosing a dinner menu and a movie. Think about military engagements, such as the ones in Iraq and Afghanistan. We have one shared military, and we must agree as a country on how to use it.

Or consider social issues like abortion. Abortion is either legal or illegal. (Those who are in favor of legalized abortion would argue that "choice" represents a policy of agreeing to disagree; their opponents would point out that the aborted fetuses do not have much choice in the matter.)

Tax policy has the same basic challenge. It is not possible to have an income tax in which everyone pays what they believe to be fair.

We have hard collective decisions to make on these kinds of issues. The notion that politicians should stop bickering and do the "right thing" makes for fine cocktail-party banter, but it is, in fact, idiotic in a public policy context. Even in the block party example, there is nothing particularly helpful about the homeowner who stands up at the planning meeting and demands, "Let's just do the right thing here!" Is that the steak or the vegetarian buffet? Is it the Disney movie or the porn film?

Different factions have profoundly different ideas about that "right thing," and there is no scientific or empirical process for choosing one over another.

All of this stands in stark contrast to the private sector, which is driven entirely by mutually beneficial *voluntary* market transactions. *No one has to agree on anything.* I like coffee; I don't need to get forty-nine other people to agree on the merits of coffee for me to walk into a Starbucks and order a cup. Similarly, Starbucks can make plenty of money by ignoring those who don't like coffee, can't afford coffee, live in countries where dictators won't let them drink coffee, have disabling diseases that prevent them from drinking coffee, and so on.

I buy coffee on any given occasion because I believe it is the very best use of my money; Starbucks makes money for its shareholders by anticipating and meeting my needs. That is all that needs to happen.

The entire private sector operates around these self-organizing transactions, and that is a great thing. But the private sector—no matter how efficient—is not going to defeat the Taliban, keep a "dirty bomb" out of the country, feed or clothe the indigent, reduce carbon emissions significantly, or do anything else to address most of our serious communal challenges.

The notion that we can or should run government like

a business is another goofy platitude that often passes for wisdom. *The whole point of government is to do things that the private sector cannot or will not do.* Businesses have the benefit of a bottom line. Success or failure can be measured with a single metric: profits. If the aforementioned block party were run like a business, all of the complexity of the decision-making would be solved with one simple analytical exercise: Which option makes us the most money? If that is a steak dinner followed by an adult-film marathon, then that is what the block party will look like. Too bad for the vegetarian families with kids.

The profit-maximizing approach is fine for Starbucks; people who do not like coffee can spend their money elsewhere. It does not work for any shared endeavor in which those who disapprove of some course of action cannot simply go elsewhere.

Public policy involves two inexorable realities: 1) We have no objective measure of the "best" course of action in many situations. 2) In such situations, many stakeholders have significantly different opinions on what the best course of action ought to be. If there is a "bottom line," it's that we can't always get what we want, particularly when most other people want something else.

It is ironic that the Tea Party has idolized the self-indulgent (and relatively easy) act of hurling tea into Boston Harbor. The truly extraordinary and unique contribution of that generation of patriots was the Constitutional Convention, which was a long, grinding series of compromises, most of which were profoundly objectionable to some faction or another.

Trade-offs and Side Effects

There are costs or trade-offs associated with everything
worth doing. This concept is obvious in private life. If you
go to college, you must pay tuition and give up income you
might have earned if you worked instead. In return for the
costs of going to college, you will get higher lifetime earn-
ings, broader career choices, or both.

If you have a serious disease, the doctor may prescribe
treatments with serious side effects, such as chemotherapy.
There is nothing good about chemotherapy, but it is a more
attractive option than dying of cancer.

Most of us get that. We understand these costs and benefits in our private lives and in business. In public policy,
however, these basic trade-offs create potential problems
because they are rarely shared equally across society. In fact,
some parties may get all of the benefits while other parties
get all of the costs. Just imagine how that would work in
the chemotherapy example. After you have been diagnosed
with cancer, the doctor walks into your room and explains
the trade-offs associated with treatment. The chemo is
highly effective, but unfortunately some guy down the hall
will lose his hair and start throwing up.

For you, the treatment decision is a no-brainer; there is
no downside. For society overall, the treatment is also worth
doing. The benefits of your cure outweigh the unpleasantness of the side effects. *And yet the guy throwing up and
losing his hair is never going to be happy about this arrangement. He is going to do everything he can to stop it.*

Sounds crazy? Here is a real example of that very phenomenon. When we expand trade with China, most Americans are made better off. We gain access to a wide array of cheap imports. We make money exporting our goods and services to the growing Chinese middle class. Overall, both countries become richer. Of course, the word *overall* is what creates the problem in that sentence. Some Americans—the workers who manufacture electronics or toys or textiles in the United States, for example—end up much worse off because of the Chinese competition. They lose their jobs and perhaps more.

This is not just a fairness issue. The workers who feel they are getting the economic equivalent of chemotherapy will march to Washington, literally or figuratively. The rest of us—those who can buy cheaper stuff at Wal-Mart—will not be paying much attention. (Does anyone ever take to the streets to protest *in favor* of more trade?) Our lawmakers will hear the screaming and nothing else. Policies that have the potential to do lots of good "overall" will die in D.C.—and rightfully so in the eyes of those who were most at risk of feeling the pain.

Even when the social costs and benefits are distributed more or less evenly across society, sensible policies often require some short-term sacrifice to move us all to a better place in the long run. We have to sweat a little before we can fit into the skinny jeans. You want to balance the federal budget? Spend less (unpopular) or tax more (also unpopular). The challenge is selling the sacrifice, not doing the math. The essence of public leadership is persuading us to get on the collective treadmill.

Unfortunately there is a lot of political mileage to be

earned by providing us plausible excuses for *not* getting on the treadmill. Why make fundamental changes to health care when we can instead reduce costs by rooting out "waste, fraud, and abuse"? We are suckers for the miracle diet, both in private and in public life (which is why very few of us fit in skinny jeans).

Worse still, we can avoid making some trade-offs in the short run because government has a unique ability to borrow from the future. Imagine a restaurant that serves fabulous, expensive food—but with a twist. At the end of the meal, the waiter brings the large check and asks if you would like to pay the bill . . . or leave it on the table for the next group of diners to pay.

You appreciate that it is not responsible to leave the bill for someone who did not share in your luxurious meal. The diners who will inherit the check have not yet arrived to make the case for why you should do the right thing. A lot of us would be tempted to leave a big chunk of that bill sitting on the table. Which is why our national debt is now seventeen trillion dollars—a giant tab that we have left on the table for future generations.

Government can do that. It is a bit of a cliché to say that we are borrowing from our children and grandchildren, but that is exactly what is going on. Every federal budget that is not balanced is another large IOU that will have to be paid by future taxpayers. One could also argue that we leave a "bill on the table" every time we raise our own standard of living by despoiling the environment in ways that will impose costs on future generations.

This is shameful, because the American way has traditionally been the opposite: leave a little extra on the table for the next generation.

There Was No Terrorist Attack Today

Thousands of planes landed safely today. Children did not choke on plastic toys. Terrorists did not strike Los Angeles. Government deserves some credit for all of those things. One inherent challenge of public policy is obvious only once you think about it: success is often invisible, or even annoying, since averting harm is not necessarily recognized as success.

Suppose that around 2005, regulators had cracked down on irresponsible mortgage lending and all of the other attendant unsavory practices that led to the global financial crisis. In 2013, would politicians, business leaders, and pundits be heaping praise on this regulatory foresight?

No. Instead, left-leaning critics would be blasting regulators for constraining credit to low-income families and denying them a piece of the American dream (with no awareness that these subprime mortgages would have turned into the American nightmare). Right-leaning critics would be blasting the same regulators for constraining the private sector and hurting profitability (with no awareness that regulators had averted a complete meltdown of the global financial system).

Do you think the CEO of Lehman Brothers would give a speech praising regulators for saving the firm from itself? Of course not, because there would be no awareness that the firm needed saving. This is a stark contrast to the private sector, where success is obvious: innovation, profits, publicity. When government works, we often see nothing but the tax bill—so it should be no great surprise that Americans across the political spectrum are not keen to send bigger checks to the government.

The High Cost of Public Service

Governing is hard. It is even harder when the job is one that no sane person would want. We have designed a system in which it is truly awful to run for public office. Raising money is a relentless, debasing process that takes time away from meaningful policy work at best, and leaves politicians indebted to their financial backers at worst. There is little public support for any kind of public funding, and the courts have repeatedly struck down campaign spending limits. According to the Center for Responsive Politics, the candidates for the House of Representatives in 2010 raised an average of $574,000 each.[23] If *you* chose to run for office, where would that $574,000 come from? Remember, you cannot legally offer your supporters any explicit quid pro quo if you win. And if you lose, they are definitely going to get nothing.

Where and how do normal people raise half a million dollars (never mind the money needed for the more expensive Senate races or the presidential campaign)? I raised roughly $400,000 in four months for my relatively short campaign during the special election in Illinois. It was an awful series of phone solicitations and fundraisers that consumed hours of every day. In one particularly frustrating moment, I literally snapped a cell phone in half. (At that point, I still needed to raise more money *and* I needed a new phone.)

We have made our beds on this one. If we continue to fund long, massively expensive campaigns this way, we cannot be shocked when our politicians are corrupted, distracted, or otherwise engaged by the pursuit of money. Nor should we be surprised when decent people decide that they have better ways to serve the public than by running for office—as if they needed one more reason.

And if they do need one more reason, do not forget that a campaign is an excuse to stir up salacious gossip. Most of this personal behavior is likely to be irrelevant to public service, but it does deter good people from running. Would you like your tax returns splayed out on the front page of the *Washington Post*, or on a Fox talk show? Would you want journalists interviewing your prom date?

Reflect for a moment on what Karl Rove (or his Democratic equivalent) could do to your life with a cleverly constructed sixty-second advertisement. You would have virtually no legal protection against what such an ad might say or insinuate.

We tolerate this abusive scrutiny because we believe that politicians are somehow different, like celebrities and pro athletes. To some extent they are, as they are seeking to inhabit positions of public trust. Still, our CEOs often enjoy similar positions of public trust without such scrutiny while making, on average, five hundred times the salary of a member of Congress. To reiterate my earlier point, the most venal and publicly destructive political

behavior, raising money from groups seeking to advance
their own narrow self-interest, is so commonplace as to be
un-newsworthy.

A political consultant once pointed out to me that the best
way to become famous is to be a rock star. The second-best
way is to become a politician. The folks looking for fame
are not necessarily the ones we want running the country.
(Former Illinois Governor Rod Blagojevich, now in prison,
comes to mind.) But these egomaniacs are the ones who will
be least deterred by the public abuse associated with the job.
We cannot expect normal people to inhabit positions that no
normal person would want.

And It Is Going to Get Harder

If you think governance is hard now, the bad news is that
it will get only tougher going forward. As a nation we have
become accustomed to a lifestyle that we cannot afford. We
have improved our quality of life by borrowing from the
future. The aforementioned national debt is seventeen trillion dollars.

For all the complaining about the cost of government, we
have literally been getting more than we have been paying
for. Forget the skinny jeans. Huge creditors like China have
allowed us to trundle around in sweatpants *and yet we are
still complaining about how tight they feel.*

To make the accounts balance going forward, we will
have to flip the inequality. Taxpayers will almost certainly
be paying more and getting less. How do you think that's
going to go over?

EDMUND BURKE, THE eighteenth-century statesman and political theorist, said famously, "All that is necessary for the triumph of evil is that good men do nothing." There is a political corollary: all that is necessary for bad governance is that sensible, well-intentioned people choose not to engage in the process. The Centrist Party is a vehicle to re-engage such people in the process, and perhaps to improve the process itself. But let's not pretend any of it will be easy.

CHAPTER 3

The Best and the Worst of the Republicans and the Democrats

DOES any informed, moderate voter who leans left really believe that America's teachers' unions are a positive force for making K–12 education better? Probably not, but those left-of-center voters still cast Democratic ballots for any number of good reasons: the Democrats are progressive on social issues, forward looking on the environment, and genuinely empathetic toward those who are struggling. There is a lot to like about the Democrats, even if it means overlooking some glaring foibles, particularly the coalition of interest groups feeding at the party trough.

Does any informed, moderate voter who leans right really believe that global warming is a scam? Probably not, but those right-of-center voters cast Republican ballots for good reasons too. The Republicans appreciate the importance of personal responsibility; they have respect for the forces that generate wealth and prosperity; they recognize that not every social problem has a government solution. Too bad the sensible small-government vision is currently intertwined with a right-wing social activism and a bizarre lack of respect for science and data. Mitt Romney was the epitome of a qualified presidential candidate compelled to say stupid things during the primaries to placate the zealots in his own party (while horrifying moderate voters). David Brooks offered a pitch-perfect assessment: "Personally, I think he's a kind, decent man who says stupid things because he is pretending to be something he is not—some sort of cartoonish government-hater."[24]

Wouldn't it be nice to have the best of both parties? What if you could walk into a voting booth and cast a ballot without having to willfully ignore the stupid things that your candidate "has to say" on the road to election? What if the tail of each party—the extremist voters who need to hear those things—could be lopped off, leaving the most sensible stuff behind?

The really good news is that both political parties have sound ideas at their core. Better yet, the most important ideas in each party are not mutually exclusive once their respective wing-nuts are cut loose. Here is a quick catalog of the best and the worst of the Republicans and the Democrats.

Thank You, Republicans

The Republicans understand and appreciate wealth creation, particularly the role of markets and trade. The only long-term path to prosperity involves harnessing the power-

ful forces of competition—and all the attendant disruptions
that come with them. The bigger the market—including
engaging economically with India, China, and the rest of
the world—the bigger the potential gains. Markets are not
perfect. After all, the flip side of innovation is disruption.
(There is nothing great about digital photography for companies that make film.) But markets are uniquely attuned
to human nature. They reward hard work, innovation, and
risk. They require relatively little centralized coordination.
And they make billions of people better off.

The Republicans understand the trade-offs associated
with taxation and regulation. Regulation raises the cost
of doing business or limits the scope of what can be done.
That is not inherently bad. The more sophisticated an economy, the more refined and complex its regulatory structure
needs to be. Still, regulation can impose a significant cost on
society, particularly when it is outdated, poorly designed, or
conceived to placate some domestic political constituency.

In the same vein, taxation diminishes the incentive to
work hard and take risks. We must reward success, not only
because that is fair in the eyes of most Americans but also
because it is best for all of us in the long run. Rich Americans are not the problem (as populist Democrats would
have us believe). *They are the solution.*

This is a crucial point as America confronts the very real
phenomenon of rising income inequality. Americans at the
bottom of the income ladder are not struggling because the
top 1 percent are getting fabulously rich; they are struggling *despite the fact that the top 1 percent are getting fabulously rich.*

The Republicans are rightfully skeptical of what government can accomplish. Not every social problem has an elegant government fix. One can care deeply about providing better opportunities for racial and ethnic minorities without necessarily embracing affirmative action. One can care deeply about public education, drug addiction, and homelessness without being convinced that throwing more money at current programs will make things better. Similarly, conservatives appreciate that government policies are prone to unintended consequences. Understanding one's limitations is an attractive personal trait for individuals; it is also an important form of modesty for governments.

As a corollary to this point, the Republicans are right to demand that individuals be held accountable for their own actions. Government cannot possibly protect us from ourselves in situations where we should know better. Government should not be responsible for supporting people who are capable of supporting themselves; people who can work should work. The notion of welfare queens driving Cadillacs has often been overstated and exploited. (Ronald Reagan's original anecdote to this effect appears to have been woven from whole cloth.) Still, anyone looking to redistribute income in the United States should appreciate a core element of the American psyche: no hardworking person likes to pay taxes to support people whom they perceive to be taking advantage of the system.

The family has to function as the basic building block of society. This is not meant to be a moral judgment; it is merely an economic and sociological reality. Even the most tightly woven safety net cannot compensate for crumbling families. Republicans are right to point with alarm to the fact that among women under the age of thirty, more than half of births are now outside of marriage, not because this is some kind of national moral failure (a fruitless and tendentious approach),* but because single-parent families are less stable economically and often have less capacity to produce successful, well-educated children.

The Republicans have a healthy respect for federalism. One of the important features of American governance is decentralization. State governments can be a source of policy innovation. More important, variation at the state level allows us to finesse ideological cleavages. People in Mississippi and Colorado may have profoundly different views on medicinal marijuana, physician-assisted suicide, or the age at which young people can get a hunting license. On many policies like this, state governments are the natural forum for compromise. National problems require federal solutions—but not all policy challenges are national in scope.

---

* Those of a certain age will remember when Dan Quayle, the conservative senator from Indiana who served as vice president under George H. W. Bush, attacked the television show *Murphy Brown* during the 1992 presidential campaign. Quayle took issue with a story line in which the show's lead character, Murphy Brown, a successful but aging single woman, decided to get pregnant and raise a child on her own. Quayle was widely mocked for criticizing the behavior of a fictional television character. On the larger issue, however, he had a point. In fact, the *Atlantic* would later run a long, in-depth cover story on the travails of single-parent families titled "Dan Quayle Was Right" (April 1993).

We should not try to agree on a federal policy when we don't have to. That is the beauty of a system with relatively powerful state and local governments.

The Republicans have historically been strong on national defense, which is inarguably a core responsibility of the federal government. (It is hard to imagine Jimmy Carter, rather than Ronald Reagan, standing in West Berlin and declaring, "Mr. Gorbachev, tear down this wall!") More recently, the same logic has been applied to antiterrorism efforts. No individual can protect against a terrorist attack or prevent a North Korean missile launch. Government is the mechanism by which we collectively protect ourselves against these kinds of potentially devastating threats. That still leaves many hard decisions regarding everything from the prison at Guantánamo Bay to Iran's nuclear program, but the core tenet is important: government must protect us from external threats.

The Republicans were, until recently, a party of fiscal restraint. The government should pay its bills and avoid passing the cost of current spending on to future generations. Large budget deficits are irresponsible, potentially destabilizing, and unfair to future taxpayers who will get the bill. This philosophy is consistent with a belief in small government, but the key point is that the accounts should balance, whether government is big, small, or somewhere in between.

What's not to like about all that? These are powerful, defensible ideas. The Republican Party I've just described embodies the core American values responsible for much of the nation's success over the past two centuries.

Thank You, Democrats

The Democrats have a lot to like as well. The Democrats rightfully believe that government can be a constructive force. It can build infrastructure, soften the edges of capitalism, empower the disadvantaged, promote education and research, and generally make our lives better than if we were left to fend for ourselves.

More specifically, the Democrats are correct to emphasize that good government makes a market economy work better. Public infrastructure—ports, roads, airports—is the domestic equivalent of national defense. Individuals cannot build the interstate highway system or improve air traffic congestion at Chicago's O'Hare airport. Similarly, government investment in basic research can lay the groundwork for the next generation of private innovation. Sensible regulation can make business transactions cheaper and more transparent. While markets are powerful forces for good, they still need adult supervision. Why would you put money in a 401(k) retirement account or buy life insurance if there were no legal assurances that the firms selling those products would not simply walk off with your money? Or to put it slightly differently, when you are stashing away hundreds of thousands of dollars for college tuitions and retirement, who scares you more: Bernie Madoff or the government officials who regulate the financial markets? As any introductory economics book would point out, good government is not the enemy of capitalism; it is a precondition.

The Democrats have a natural empathy for the truly

disadvantaged. Every one of the world's major faiths has a core belief built around the notion that society has an obligation to help those who are in need. Jesus did not call for lower taxes on prosperous merchants so that their growing wealth would eventually trickle down and provide bread and fishes for the starving.

We live in the richest nation in the history of human civilization; no sentient person can believe it is truly okay that some of our fellow citizens are eating out of trash cans, or that 20 percent of all children are living in poverty. These problems turn out to be shockingly difficult to solve, and traditional Democratic solutions are not necessarily as effective as they might be, but the Democrats have their hearts in the right place—and that matters. Caring about social problems is a precondition for solving them.

More recently, the Democrats have been correct to engage on the issue of income inequality. Again, many of the solutions are half-baked; this is not a situation that can be addressed with redistribution alone. Still, the Democrats are correct in thinking that the social fabric of the country will be corroded if the people on Main Street come to believe that the system is rigged in favor of the elites on Wall Street (and elsewhere). The problem is not necessarily the widening gap between the 99 percent and the 1 percent, but the growing belief that the 1 percent have pulled up the ladder behind them. The American ideal will collapse if citizens across the income spectrum no longer believe that the people at the top have earned it and that every citizen has a shot at ending up on top.

America has never promised great outcomes for all, but it has always promised equal opportunity. At their best, the Democrats understand that when poor children are stuck in lousy schools, or when middle-class families cannot afford college, we are not fulfilling that promise. The Democrats are also right to focus on "rent seeking" by the very rich—the notion that the most privileged Americans (such as Wall Street bankers) are using their political clout to enrich and protect themselves in ways that make the rest of us worse off. There is no doubt that the 2008 financial crisis was caused in part by a regulatory system that allowed financial firms to earn staggering profits when times were good while leaving the government with the tab for huge private losses when the party was over. That is not how markets are supposed to work.

The Democrats have been more aggressive in protecting the rights of gays, minorities, the disabled, and other groups outside the mainstream. The Republicans may be the party of Lincoln, but Abe would be ashamed at the party's current intolerance. America has become a steadily more inclusive nation; the credit in recent decades belongs almost exclusively to those who lean left.

The Democrats have a far better record of protecting the environment. On that issue, they are right both substantively and, in the long run, politically. Again, any introductory economics book makes the crucial point that markets *do not work efficiently* when private behavior generates costs that spill over and harm the rest of us—like air and water pollution. When markets do not send accurate price signals (e.g., when the private cost of producing electricity from coal does not include the cost of CO_2 emissions), the "invisible hand" no longer points in a sensible direction. This is an overly technical explanation of what most Americans understand intuitively: private firms should not have free rein to do things that harm public health and well-being. Climate change makes the stakes all the higher in that regard.

The Democrats are not effective in communicating their environmental message (Al Gore's Oscar award notwithstanding), and the policies they advocate are not particularly well designed. But public opinion with regard to the environment will continue to move steadily in the Democrats' direction. Younger voters care more about environmental issues than older voters do. And wealthier countries (and wealthier people within any particular country) typically place a higher priority on protecting the environment than those who are struggling economically, in large part because their other needs have been met.

The future is clear. Environmental issues will grow ever more important in voters' eyes as younger generations assume the mantle of power, as the nation grows steadily richer, and as the evidence on climate change becomes harder and harder to ignore.

What's not to like about all that? The Democrats rightfully recognize that good government has an invaluable role to play in wealth creation. By making shared investments that promote markets and productivity, and by softening the rough edges of American capitalism, Democratic policies can make our system more durable and inclusive.

Back to Reality

Someone walking into the voting booth with a choice between the two parties I have just described would be extremely fortunate. At their best, the Republicans and the Democrats stand for two perfectly reasonable worldviews. Neither is "right"; both are defensible. Anyone who leans modestly left should still be able to appreciate what Republicans care about and why they feel that way. The same is true looking in the other direction.

Obviously there are tensions between each party's key priorities. Protecting the environment (a legitimate Democratic objective) places some constraints on economic growth and wealth creation (an important Republican objective). Building infrastructure and protecting our most vulnerable citizens requires a bigger, more activist government, which is a hard sell for small-government conservatives. And so on.

There is no miracle elixir here. Still, if Congress were full of pragmatic Democrats and Republicans whose intellectually honest views embodied the best of each party, we could navigate these trade-offs. The natural compromises would strike most American voters as perfectly reasonable.

But Congress is not made up of politicians who represent the best of each party. The tragedy of American politics— which has become the tragedy of America—is that these partisan members have an agenda of their own that is a bastardization of most of what I have just described.

When political candidates emerge from a Republican or Democratic primary (having just placated the "base"), what those candidates do, say, and stand for bears little resemblance to all the important ideals I have just described. Here is what we get instead.

The Democrats We Have Come to Know

The current Democratic Party is too skeptical of business, too hostile toward wealth creation, and overly abusive of America's most productive citizens—often because there are votes to be had by poking the rich in the eye. Yes, a modern economy needs regulation, but that regulation needs to be targeted and have minimal costs. Like a good physician, we want to fix the problem—because there are problems that need government fixes—without messing anything else up.

We do not have to call anyone a "fat cat" while doing this. After all, even "fat cats" do not like to be called "fat cats"—and business leaders who are working very, very hard to hold their firms together during a prolonged economic slump *really* do not like being falsely demonized for the nation's problems.

The Democrats too often oppose trade, outsourcing, and other wealth-creating elements of a modern global economy. These are things that make the world richer and more productive. They lift hundreds of millions of people out of poverty around the globe; they deliver innovation and cheaper goods (which effectively raises the incomes of poor Americans). Trade and outsourcing, like all market activities, also create losers. The reality of a capitalist economy is that whenever someone develops a better mousetrap—

whether it comes from Shanghai or Seattle—the factory
that produced the old mousetrap must close or lay off workers. That is how markets work.

But rather than fixing the rough edges of capitalism—
cleaning up after the golden goose—the Democrats too
often threaten to skewer the goose and feed it to the angry
mob. The sad irony is that the party demagogues are standing in the way of economic growth that would provide enormous benefit for the American middle class over the long
run. Paul Tsongas, the Democratic senator from Massachusetts who ran for president in 1992, delivered a stinging
critique of his own party that still rings true twenty years
later. He declared, "You can't be pro-jobs and anti-business,"
which would appear to be a statement of the obvious.[25] Yet
the Democrats still refuse to read that memo.

In the same vein, the Democrats have a bias for government action that rests on the belief that doing something is always better than doing nothing. They are not
unlike the peddlers of patent medicines who traversed
the American frontier in the nineteenth century, claiming
they could cure every toothache or goiter with the right
foul-smelling concoction of dried roots and grain alcohol.
If only that were true.

The Democrats have clung too long to ham-handed policies that are not doing what they are supposed to do. The
intention is almost always good, but there is too little recognition that implementing a program is not synonymous
with solving a problem. (In contrast, the Republicans are
masters of pretending that many serious problems simply
do not exist.)

The Democrats have been far too slow to recognize that our entitlement programs need to be updated. The only way to save Social Security and Medicare is to make them financially solvent for the long run. And since reforming entitlements is a prerequisite for fixing the federal budget, the Democrats are essentially AWOL when it comes to restoring the country to fiscal sanity. The party will not shed its "tax and spend" reputation until it gets serious about entitlement reform.

Rather than putting together policies that make ideological sense and have broad appeal to voters, the Democrats have gone looking for prospective voters and then crafted policies to appeal to those groups. As a result, the party has gradually become a collection of interest groups rather than a group of interests coalescing around a coherent intellectual approach to policy.

One of those crucial Democratic voting blocs is organized labor—which has done a terrific job of delivering votes, raising cash, *and robbing the party of its intellectual legitimacy*. Being pro-union is *not* synonymous with being pro-worker in an economy where private firms have to be flexible and competitive and governments must reduce costs. The right to organize is a fundamental American right that has delivered important gains for American workers for more than a century; organized labor still has that potential. But too many unions have advocated self-serving policies that are not good for the overall economy—and not even in the best long-term interests of the workers they purport to represent.

No group has done more to diminish the status of the teaching profession than its biggest union, the National

Education Association. Are public school teachers important? Yes. Do they work hard? Yes. But those teachers cannot
expect society to look at them as if they were doctors and
judges (and pay them accordingly) while they are demanding contracts more appropriate for a 1930s steel worker—
rigid hours, guaranteed employment, uniform pay based
on seniority rather than performance, and so on.

Rather than systematically working to improve the plight
of American workers, the U.S. labor movement got stuck
somewhere around 1950—before there was intense pressure to compete with foreign firms, to restrain government
spending, and to improve our schools. For the United States
to succeed economically, labor needs to be an active partner
in all of these endeavors. Instead, unions have opposed trade
agreements, opposed charter schools, opposed tax reform
(to protect the tax exemption for generous fringe benefits),
opposed merit pay for teachers, opposed reforms to government procurement, and opposed many other commonsense
changes that would make Main Street Americans—the
bread and butter of the Democratic Party—better off.

The Scary Republicans

For all that, those who lean right should not be smug,
because when the Republican Party is bad, it is really,
really bad. The party's fundamental problem stems from
the fact that the Republicans are not really one party at all;
they are two.

First, there are the traditional conservatives, in the literal
sense of the word, who believe in small government and low

taxes. They typically have a libertarian view when it comes to social issues. Part of "small government" is leaving citizens alone in their private behavior. One should not forget that Barry Goldwater, father of the modern conservative movement, was pro-choice, as was Ayn Rand, the libertarian author extolled by so many current Republican leaders.

Second, there are the radical right-wingers, as embodied by the Tea Party. This group has an almost pathological aversion to taxes and government. However, these so-called social conservatives (a complete misnomer) simultaneously support an aggressive and activist government *on issues they believe in*: forbidding people of the same sex from getting married; ensuring that schoolchildren pray in public schools; locking up suspected terrorists without trial or legal representation; forbidding a woman from terminating a pregnancy; spending tremendous amounts of public money on the military; and so on. One can agree or disagree with any of these positions, but let's not pretend that they represent limited government.

It is a strange crew inside the Republican tent, as the small-government libertarians mingle with the social-engineering right-wingers. The Republican candidates who stagger out of that awkwardly big tent these days (e.g., Mitt Romney) are usually dragging a lot of baggage with them. The best of the Republican Party often gets lost in the process.

The traditional (and healthy) Republican skepticism of what government can reasonably accomplish has morphed into a general hostility toward all government programs (with the very expensive exception of defense). Taxes are bad, like some kind of disease to be avoided, and tax cuts are always good. This simple-minded view has supplanted the more sensible perspective that taxes are more like a vaccine—when used appropriately, they have the potential to deliver benefits far in excess of the unpleasantness.

The 2012 Republican presidential primary presented one particularly absurd example: all of the major candidates vowed to veto a hypothetical budget that contained ten dollars in spending cuts for every one dollar in tax increases. Any intellectually honest fiscal conservative will tell you that America would have been lucky to get such a bargain.

When Republicans cling to the anti-tax, anti-government dogma, they are *not* asking the more subtle and important questions that should be coming from the party of small government: What is the role of government? What kinds of taxes do the least harm to the economy? Might the costs of higher taxes be offset by the benefits of getting America's fiscal house in order, particularly if it is part of a grand bargain to cut spending and reform the tax code? And so on.

The companion problem is that the Republicans have held the line on taxes but not on spending. The largest expansion of the American entitlement system since Lyndon Johnson's Great Society was Medicare Part D, which created prescription drug coverage for seniors. The bill was passed by the Republican-controlled House, with "yes" votes from supposed fiscal hawks like Paul Ryan and Eric Cantor, and signed into law by a Republican president, George W. Bush.

Is prescription drug coverage an important supplement

to medical coverage for Americans over the age of sixty-five? Perhaps. But taking an already unaffordable Medicare program and making it larger is most definitely not small government.

Paul Ryan also voted against the Simpson-Bowles deficit-reduction recommendations, a package of sensible spending cuts and tax increases—negotiated by a bipartisan commission—that would have put the country back on the road to fiscal sanity. He opposed the bipartisan compromises because he refused to countenance *any* tax increases and because the plan did not go far enough to address rising health-care costs. Okay. But in holding out for a whole loaf, Ryan and other Republican ideologues ended up with no budget deal at all. A serious problem just got worse.

Then there are the wars, which do not come at small-government prices. The Iraq War will cost American taxpayers approximately one trillion dollars by the time all the various expenses are tallied up. That could have funded a lot of roads, bridges, teachers, and basic research. Invading Iraq may or may not have been the right thing to do, but either way, we spent a staggering sum doing it. There seems to be a mental game that Republicans play in which defense spending does not count as big government, even as the United States spends more on defense than all of our allies combined.

Here is a fascinating economic insight: *Government spending is when the government spends money.* On anything. Whether it is to pay soldiers in Afghanistan or unemployed steel workers in Pennsylvania, taxpayers still get the bill. The taxes that support national defense have the same adverse effect on the economy as the taxes that support domestic spending programs, most of which are much, much, much smaller in scale and far more likely to promote productivity and prosperity in America.

The Republicans are also the party of big government when it comes to social issues. In a 2003 decision (*Lawrence v. Texas*), the Supreme Court invalidated a Texas antisodomy law because it violated the constitutional right to privacy. Republican right-wingers railed against the decision.

Let's reflect on that for a moment. One does not have to be a rabid proponent of sodomy to understand that those purporting to favor small government should not be in the business of legislating which private sexual behavior is legal and which is not. As the British news magazine *The Economist* noted when right-wing activist Rick Santorum placed second in the Iowa presidential caucuses, "Now is the time for consenting adults to lock their bedroom doors."[26]

The Republicans are just plain wrong on environmental policy. Basic economics—the same study of markets that conservatives typically extol—tells us that most environmental problems are "market failures," meaning that producers and consumers do not take the cost of pollution into account when they are making private decisions. This is one of those relatively rare circumstances in which markets do not align private behavior in ways that are consistent with what is good for society overall. As a result, economists across the political spectrum have embraced pollution taxes, such as a carbon tax, as a better way to raise government revenue than taxing productive activities like work, savings, and investment.

Gary Becker—a Nobel Prize winner from the University of Chicago, a disciple of Milton Friedman, and one of the most articulate contemporary proponents of free markets— is on record as favoring a carbon tax. So is former Federal Reserve chairman Alan Greenspan (who was a close friend of Ayn Rand while she was alive). Another persistent and persuasive advocate for some kind of carbon tax is Harvard economist Gregory Mankiw, who is the author of one of the most popular economics textbooks in America. More important in this context, Mankiw was the chair of the Council of Economic Advisers under George W. Bush.

The Booth School of Business at the University of Chicago polled an ideologically diverse group of prominent economists about their views on a carbon tax; *96 percent* of the economists polled answered either "agree" or "strongly agree" that a twenty-dollar-per-ton tax on carbon emissions would be better for the U.S. economy than an income tax increase that raised the same amount of revenue ($150 billion annually).[27]

Why do economists, including conservatives such as Mankiw, advocate for putting a price on carbon? Because raising the cost of carbon-based fuels by a modest amount would encourage conservation and promote cleaner alternatives without the government having to offer expensive subsidies (e.g., ethanol) or to pick technological winners (e.g., Solyndra, the California-based manufacturer of solar panels that received large federal subsidies before going bankrupt).

Think about it: If we tax income, people work less. If we tax carbon, they pollute less. You don't have to win the Nobel Prize in economics to understand that logic (though to reiterate, those who *have* won the Nobel Prize are particularly likely to feel this way).

More generally, the Tea Party conservatives and their right-wing brethren tend to have a theological view of governance that is oddly impervious to facts and data. If the facts do not support a particular policy or position, then it is the facts that have to be discarded, not the policy. That is a dangerous approach to science-based issues like evolution and climate change. On the economic front, the same triumph of belief over data has enabled leading Republicans to cling to the discredited notion that we can increase the amount of revenue that the government collects by cutting taxes.* A colleague of mine who served in the George W. Bush administration describes this enduring canard as "faith-based economics." Despite that faith, whenever taxes have gone down in recent times, deficits have gone up.

Nothing encapsulates the triumph of belief over fancy-

---

* In June of 2012, the Booth School of Business at the University of Chicago asked the same ideologically diverse group of expert economists mentioned earlier to agree or disagree with the following statement: "A cut in federal income tax rates in the US right now would raise taxable income enough so that the annual total tax revenue would be higher within five years than without the tax cut." When the answers were weighted by the respondent's confidence in his or her answer, 96 percent said "disagree" or "strongly disagree"; 4 percent said "uncertain." Not a single expert answered "agree" or "strongly agree." ("Laffer Curve," Initiative on Global Markets, IGM Forum, Chicago Booth, June 26, 2012, http://www.igmchicago.org/igm-economic-experts-panel/poll-results? SurveyID=SV_2irlrss5UC27YXi)

pants experts and their "data" better than Karl Rove's 2012 Election Night meltdown on Fox News. When the Fox statisticians—the nerds who were literally cloistered in a back room—called Ohio (and therefore the election) for Obama, Rove refused to accept their analysis. When we want something to be true (or false) badly enough, why should we let empirical evidence get in the way?

Meanwhile, the ideological purity demanded by the right wing of the Republican Party has made compromise a nonstarter. During the summer of 2011, Congress convened a "super committee" to negotiate a bipartisan plan for addressing the looming fiscal crisis. A Gallup poll conducted at the time found that a solid majority of Americans were willing to embrace a compromise solution, even if it included things they did not agree with. Sixty percent of American adults supported compromise, including 55 percent of self-described Republicans, 57 percent of independents, and 67 percent of Democrats. There was one exception: the Tea Party.[28]

The same poll found that 53 percent of Americans self-identifying as Tea Party members said they would advise committee members sharing their beliefs to "hold out for a plan you would agree with, even if it prevents the committee from reaching an agreement." Many of you will recognize this approach from childhood, when the spoiled kid down the block threatened to take his football and go home if he could not play quarterback.

The purpose of this book is to create a new political alternative, not to allocate blame between the two parties. Still, it is worth pointing out that the ideological rigidity of the current Republican Party has made it particularly hard to govern a large and diverse country. Thomas Mann and Norman Ornstein, scholars from opposite sides of the political spectrum who have studied Congress for decades, blame a dysfunctional Republican Party for much of the current stalemate in Washington. In their book *It's Even Worse Than It Looks*, Mann and Ornstein write, "The Republican Party has become an insurgent outlier—ideologically extreme; contemptuous of the inherited social and economic policy regime; scornful of compromise; unpersuaded by conventional understanding of facts, evidence, and science; and dismissive of the legitimacy of its political opposition."[29]

Remember, there is a lot to like about a conservative party that advocates for small government and understands what markets can accomplish and what they cannot. The problem is that the Republicans are not that party right now.

A Pox on Both Their Houses

The current political culture in Washington makes everything I have just described worse. Given a choice between political victory and fixing real problems, our politicians have consistently chosen the former. If that seems like an exaggeration, let's look at the 2011 battle over the debt ceiling. By way of background, whenever the United States reaches its borrowing limit as allowed by law, Congress must vote to raise the limit and allow additional federal borrowing. This is largely a pro forma vote, as the spending decisions have already been made. The debt ceiling vote merely allows the government to borrow sufficient funds to continue paying its bills. If for some reason the debt ceiling were not raised, the United States could technically default on some of its debt—a risky outcome that could dangerously destabilize financial markets.

The debt ceiling vote is important but largely symbolic. If the opposition party in Congress were to deny a sitting president an increase in the debt ceiling, the result would be potentially catastrophic. Thus, it is a powerful if somewhat reckless bargaining chip. When politicians threaten to vote against raising the debt ceiling, it is the fiscal equivalent of putting a gun to the head of the country. *Give me exactly what I want, or I'll pull the trigger and send the global financial system into chaos.* (This is what spoiled children who threaten to take their footballs home do when they become adults.)

And it is what the Republicans did in the spring of 2011 when the federal government was set to hit its $14.3 trillion borrowing limit. Since the Republicans controlled the House of Representatives, they could hold President Obama hostage by threatening to throw the United States into default if they did not get other things that they wanted. The more credible their threat, the more dangerous it became. The whole endeavor was good for partisan politicians and bad for the country. Shame on the Republicans.

But wait: The Republicans are not the only ones playing this game. As a senator, Barack Obama voted against raising the debt ceiling while George W. Bush was president. Shame on the Democrats too.

Gerald Seib, author of the Capital Journal column for

the *Wall Street Journal*, has observed, "Few exercises produce as much cynical and overtly partisan behavior by elected officials as do votes on the debt ceiling." In a clever exercise, Seib examined the voting records of Iowa's two U.S. senators, Republican Charles Grassley and Democrat Tom Harkin. Each senator had voted seven times on bills to raise the debt ceiling since 2002. Here is what Seib found: "Every time a Republican president has needed the debt ceiling raised to keep government functioning, Mr. Grassley, the Republican, has voted to raise it while the Democrat, Mr. Harkin, has voted against it. But when a Democratic president has asked for an increase, their votes reverse: Mr. Harkin has voted in favor, and Mr. Grassley has voted against it."[30]

In Washington, with our two entrenched, ossified parties, all of this passes as business as usual. The goal is to shaft the other party—even if it shafts the country too—because that is how each party claws its way to more electoral power. The obvious problem is that with both parties chronically acting that way, we are perpetually taking sensible compromises off the table *because that might make the other party look good.*

In the fall of 2011, when the budget "super committee" failed to reach an agreement on a fiscal plan, political scientists Amy Gutmann and Dennis Thompson offered a less crude explanation for this "toxic partisan gridlock." They wrote in the *New York Times*, "The [super committee] exercise proved that the capital is caught in a centrifuge that allows those with an uncompromising mind-set to

chase the tantalizing partisan dream: My party will gain
control, and push through its agenda, undiluted."[31]

How is that working out for us?

THERE IS A better way. We will cut loose the ideological
tails and combine the best of the Republicans and Democrats into a pragmatic party committed to solving America's problems.

That is the Centrist Party.

CHAPTER 4

The Centrist Party

THE Centrist Party must be more than a collection of people who are *not* Republicans or Democrats. It will be organized around principles drawn from the best of the two traditional parties, with some Tea Party passion thrown in.

We must promote prosperity and productivity by respecting the power of markets and trade. We should harness the power of competition whenever possible, including in the provision of public services like education. We must reform our public spending—and our entitlement programs in particular—before America's debt burden becomes unmanageable. We can refine the tax and regulatory structure to promote hard work and investment.

None of that should suggest that government is an inherently bad thing. We need infrastructure, public safety, and protection from terrorists and rogue nuclear states. We must invest in education. We must reinvigorate the social compact so that any citizen who works hard and follows the rules can reasonably hope to join the middle class. We must fix a health-care system that is unsustainably expensive and produces shockingly mediocre health outcomes. We need a sensible and predictable regulatory structure *to make markets work better.* Good government can and should provide the tracks on which the engine of capitalism runs.

We should proudly (if not necessarily eagerly) pay for all of this with an efficient and reasonably progressive tax system because, as former Supreme Court justice Oliver Wendell Holmes pointed out, "Taxes are the price we pay for a civilized society."

We should respect the rights of individuals and, to the extent possible, finesse our deep ideological disagreements on social issues by keeping government out of our private lives. When that is not possible, we should search for pragmatic compromises (e.g., reducing the number of abortions rather than conducting scorched-earth campaigns over every Supreme Court nominee).

At the same time, we must demand responsibility from every citizen. A society that offers a meaningful safety net has a right to ask certain things of its citizens in return. It is *not* okay to drop out of school, or to have a child whom one cannot support financially and emotionally, or to engage in any other behavior with large social costs that redound to the rest of society. This is not a morality judgment; it is economic reality. The only way to build a stable prosperous society is on a foundation of responsible individuals and families.

Obviously government cannot *make* people behave responsibly, but policies can be designed with an expectation that those who can afford to help themselves should be doing so: paying for college, saving for retirement, buying appropriate insurance, and so on. Government can make all of this easier, and it should offer help to those who genuinely need it, but we cannot afford to have government as the social service provider of first resort.

When individuals do seek public assistance, as is inevitable, we have a right to ask reasonable things in return: looking for work, returning to school, participating in substance abuse treatment, or doing other things that minimize the long-term public burden. I will be the first to concede how hard this is to do well (and that doing it badly can make things worse). There is a Nobel Prize waiting for anyone who designs a program that consistently redirects the lives of sixteen-year-old high school dropouts. The point here is philosophical: there is nothing wrong with "strings attached" when it comes to social welfare programs.

Overall, these principles present a framework for public decision-making around which moderate, pragmatic people can rally. Nothing here will make the fundamental challenges of governing go away. Nothing here will resolve basic and honest ideological disagreements, such as whether life begins at conception or what a wealthy country owes its most disadvantaged citizens.

Yet there is widespread political agreement among moderate Americans on a wide range of issues that continue to paralyze our nation. If the political middle—those who care more about making a difference than making noise—can coalesce around a basic approach, then we have a good start.

How might this work in practice? We watched it happen in 2010 with the Simpson-Bowles deficit-reduction commission I mentioned earlier. President Obama appointed this bipartisan, eighteen-person National Commission on Fiscal Responsibility and Reform to address the nation's fiscal challenges. The co-chairs were Alan Simpson, a former Republican senator from Wyoming, and Erskine Bowles, a Democrat and Bill Clinton's former chief of staff. The commission produced a long list of spending cuts, tax increases, and entitlement reforms that were widely applauded by policy analysts and economists across the political spectrum. The commission's recommendations represented a pragmatic, bipartisan first step toward restoring fiscal sanity in America.

So what happened? President Obama did not embrace or endorse the commission's findings. He opted not to use his bully pulpit to sell our country on some unpleasant but necessary medicine, or even to use the Simpson-Bowles proposals as a starting point for negotiations.

Nancy Pelosi, the Democratic Speaker of the House at the time, rejected the plan because of its spending cuts, particularly the changes to Social Security.

The Republicans balked at the tax increases, such as the proposed increase in the gas tax. As previously noted, Representative Paul Ryan, the alleged Republican go-to guy on fiscal issues, was a member of the deficit commission but voted against its final recommendations.

The sensible Simpson-Bowles recommendations had no meaningful support from either party. The plan landed in Washington like a dead fish.

Here is the tragedy: *a majority of Americans supported the sensible recommendations of the Simpson-Bowles commission.* Even with the tough love—a higher gas tax, a higher retirement age for Social Security, a reduction in the home mortgage-interest deduction, and other real sacrifices—American voters were willing to compromise in a way that their representatives were not. A Gallup poll taken shortly after the Simpson-Bowles recommendations were released found that 60 percent of Americans were willing to support a deficit reduction compromise even if it was a plan that they "personally disagreed with."[32]

In other words, our current political system failed to confront our enormous fiscal challenges, *not because of what voters wanted, but despite it.* The fundamental role of the Centrist Party is twofold: 1) to introduce pragmatic policies like the Simpson-Bowles recommendations that represent sane solutions to serious problems; and 2) to change the structure of national politics so that these kind of sensible ideas do not die in a Congress that is far more partisan than the American electorate.

WHAT POLICIES WOULD a group of one hundred well-informed reasonable people agree on if the radical right- and left-wingers were locked outside the room, banging on the door trying to get in?

Let's start there.

The Centrist Party Principles and Goals

Government should do what individuals and businesses cannot do. The whole point of government is to do things that make its citizens collectively better off. No individual can police the borders to intercept terrorists. No individual can protect the water quality in the Great Lakes. And no private firm will perform these valuable services because there is no way to collect a fee from the "free riders" who benefit from the outcome but can refuse to pay. (How exactly would a firm improve the water quality in the Great Lakes or hunt terrorists *only for its paying customers?*)

Government can make markets work better; government can provide valuable goods and services that the market will not; and government can improve on market outcomes when private behavior causes significant social damage. The Centrist view of government is rooted in basic economics—understanding what markets do well and what they do not—rather than rigid ideology.

Individuals should do what government cannot (or should not) do. We can and should apply the same economic logic to determine what government *does not need to do*, namely, the things that individuals and private firms can do better on their own. Government does not need to subsidize the mortgages of middle- and upper-class citizens, or to pay farmers to turn corn into ethanol, or to protect informed consumers from themselves, or to interfere in the private behavior of consenting adults.

When private behavior does not affect the rest of us,

we ought to let individuals decide what is appropriate and what is not. This leads to what might be perceived as a "liberal" view on social issues such as gay marriage and drug use. True enough. But it also means that citizens who want to keep a gun in their home for self-defense ought to be able to do so. (Once they take the gun outside, or sell it to a street gang, then it becomes our business.)

The corollary to devolving authority to individuals and families is that we ought to expect responsible behavior in exchange for a more tightly woven social safety net. When individuals are unable or unwilling to support themselves or their dependents, the rest of us are left with the bill. A rich country should pay those bills when they avert human misery. *However, a social contract, like every contract, must ask something of both parties.* Government should provide for those who fall through the cracks, but the first line of defense against such deprivation is to urge citizens to walk as far away from those cracks as possible.

Align policy to create wealth and promote productivity. The bigger the pie, the easier everything else becomes. The first order of business is taking full advantage of America's remarkable economic potential.

More specifically:

√ **Respect markets.** Markets align incentives in ways that maximize our human potential. We work harder when we get to keep more (as the Soviet Union learned the hard way). Every Centrist policy should be viewed through this lens.

We should harness the power of the market to address some of our public challenges. Students should have choices among schools. Government should collaborate with the private sector to build and operate infrastructure. Public programs should make use of private contractors if they can deliver services more affordably and efficiently.

At the same time we ought to recognize that markets are fabulously powerful *even when we would prefer otherwise*. The same politicians who rightfully praise the genius and power of markets have waged a failing "war on drugs" for three decades. It is time to revisit the naïve belief that government can somehow permanently disrupt the flow of illicit drugs with a strategy that relies primarily on interdiction.

To paraphrase the serenity prayer, the Centrist Party will respect the power of markets when they work well, tweak the outcomes when they do not, and have the wisdom always to tell the difference.

√   **Promote free trade.** Free trade is nothing more than markets that happen to cross international borders. The exchange of goods and services between the United States and China creates wealth for the same reasons that trade between California and New York does. We ought to promote free trade because it makes us collectively richer, and because it is the most powerful force for ameliorating poverty and deprivation around the world. Of course, the uncomfortable reality is that trade disrupts life too—just like domestic economic competition does. To that end, two other principles are crucial to this focus on free trade: building skills and providing a meaningful social safety net.

√ **Invest in human capital.** Our nation must have a strategy for investing in human capital at every stage in life. This should literally start at birth with targeted, high-quality early childhood education. The evidence is overwhelming that early childhood education has a profound impact on future success, particularly for children from disadvantaged families.

We must dramatically upgrade our K–12 education system, which is at the heart of our efforts to create productive citizens. This is an admittedly difficult task; thirty years of various reform efforts (from both the political right and left) have generated mostly disappointing results. Still, the system must get better. We cannot have 25 percent of our students dropping out of high school at a time when even a high school diploma does not guarantee economic security.

We must invest in our colleges and universities, which have historically been one of our greatest engines of growth, innovation, and prosperity. We must also invest in an array of programs that supplement traditional higher education: job training, community colleges, specialized appren-

ticeships, re-training opportunities for workers
made redundant later in life, and so on.

The point is not that education and skills guarantee lifetime employment. They do not. High-
skilled people get laid off all the time: professional
baseball managers, Wall Street CEOs, Lindsay
Lohan's publicists. The key is that highly skilled
individuals are more productive, more adaptable,
and more economically resilient. They are also
better parents and better citizens. The benefit of
investing in skills is a more resilient and productive workforce, which in turn creates a richer and
more resilient nation. This "up-skilling" is also
the only realistic long-term strategy for strength-
ening the American middle class, which finds
itself under siege from technology, outsourcing,
trade, immigration, and other forces that are putting jobs at risk and holding down wages.

Government does not have to pay for all this.
There are enormous private gains to education; it
is perfectly reasonable to expect most Americans
to invest in their own futures. Nor should government have a monopoly on providing education
and training. Too many of our public institutions
(and many private institutions) do a shockingly
poor job of providing relevant skills in a timely
and cost-effective manner. Still, government must
oversee the system: providing standards, offering
financial aid to those who would otherwise be
denied access to education or training, investing

in basic research, demanding that every citizen achieve some minimum level of education, and generally ensuring that Americans are educated to their fullest potential.

√ **Build and maintain twenty-first-century infrastructure.** A successful society needs to move people, goods, and information. Individuals cannot build their own air traffic control systems. Private firms do not have the power of eminent domain to create new corridors for moving freight and information.

Our nation needs an infrastructure strategy that lays out the most important federal infrastructure goals (e.g., reducing traffic congestion, improving air quality, promoting Internet connectivity, etc.) and then creates a mechanism for evaluating all federal projects against those goals. The most cost-effective projects should be included in the infrastructure budget; the projects that do not meet some threshold for cost-effectiveness should be rejected.

Earmarks, the process by which individual legislators tuck their pet projects into larger bills, will not disappear entirely. Congress has the power to pass legislation, including legislation that spends money on stupid things. However, an objective set of criteria for evaluating transportation projects would quantify the silliness of these pet projects. If modernizing the nation's air traffic control system scores 91 out of 100 when it is evaluated against federal transportation goals, and expanding the parking lot at the Lawn Darts Hall of Fame scores a 3, then it becomes all the more shameful to spend money on the latter. And when shame does not work, a presidential veto just might.

This basic approach has two major advantages. First, it can help restore public trust in the government's ability to make sensible infrastructure investments—rather than allowing "bridges to nowhere" to be built because an influential legislator was able to slip an earmark into the transportation bill. Second, it provides a less controversial and more efficient form of "stimulus" during economic downturns. Once the federal government has an infrastructure plan made up of approved projects, it is possible to reach deeper into that list of "shovel-ready projects" during slack economic times. *There is no money wasted on stimulus spending; sensible spending is merely speeded up.*

√ **Design a more efficient tax system.** Taxes do two things: they raise revenue *and they change behavior*. Our public discussions about tax policy tend to focus almost exclusively on the former. How much is the government taking out of each of our pockets? Which candidate is going to raise my taxes? The behavioral incentives created by taxation deserve far more attention. If we tax gasoline, people drive less. If we tax capital gains, people invest less. Both of those taxes raise revenue, but they obviously have markedly different impacts on society.

One of the fundamental rules of public finance is that governments should tax activities they would like to discourage. *Working, saving, and investing do not fall in that category*, yet these are the activities that our current system taxes most heavily. Given our environmental challenges, particularly climate change, the United States ought to lean more heavily on "green taxes," such as a carbon tax. Taxing pollution raises revenues so that we can tax productive activities more lightly—like working, saving, and investing. There is ample room to improve the incentives embedded in the tax code while ensuring that the overall system remains reasonably progressive.

At the same time, the current corporate and income tax systems are riddled with needless complexity. Closing dubious loopholes makes it possible to generate the same amount of revenue with lower rates. The result is a simpler and fairer tax code. Of course, as logical as tax reform may appear, the politics are surprisingly difficult. Even the most absurd tax exemptions put money in someone's pocket; the individuals and firms who benefit from our current maze of complexity will fight to keep their preferred treatment. The goal of the Centrist Party must be to face down narrow interests and build a tax system that strengthens the country overall.

√ **Promote labor relations 2.0.** The American labor market has changed profoundly over the last two decades; by and large, the American labor movement has not. There is still a role to play for unions in many sectors of the economy. The right to organize is a basic and important freedom. But organized labor, in both the public and the private sector, must become a partner in promoting productivity and innovation rather than an obstacle.

Traditional labor unions have pitted workers against management in an adversarial, zero-sum relationship. The whole approach assumes that there is some fixed pot of resources to be split between the two sides and that getting more of that pot is always the optimal strategy. For a long time, this basic approach served American workers well. (One of my favorite bumper stickers reads, "Unions: The people who brought you the weekend.") The problem is that the labor movement has not adapted to a twenty-first-century economy in which the firms employing organized labor face increasing competitive pressures, both from foreign companies and from non-unionized firms in the United States. The assumption that labor and management are bargaining over a fixed pot of wealth is now dangerously wrong. *Labor and management are involved in a shared enterprise*

*that could shrink or grow depending on strategic
decisions, many of which involve how labor is put
to work.*

Firms need to be flexible. They need to cut
costs continuously. They need to source materials
as cheaply and efficiently as possible. If all of this
is not happening, the business is not viable in the
long run. Labor and management must collaborate to grow (or protect) their pot of wealth; only
then should they argue over the split.

On this point, the Hostess Twinkie can provide
a valuable lesson. In the fall of 2012, Hostess and
one of its major unions could not come to agreement on wage concessions to keep the company
profitable. The people who bake our Ho Hos (are
they actually baked?) went on strike. The bakers'
union, like the rest of us, did not want their wages
cut. Here's the problem: Hostess ended up closing
its doors for good. No more Twinkies, Ho Hos,
Devil Dogs, or Wonder Bread (though the brands
could be sold in liquidation).

And no more jobs for 18,500 workers.[33]

The last gasp of the old-guard labor movement has been the public-sector unions, which are
largely insulated from the competitive pressures I
just described. For decades, higher costs could be
passed along to taxpayers or covered with long-
term borrowing. The music has stopped on this
arrangement. Many state and local governments
are now groaning under the cost of unafford-

able and inflexible labor contracts and extravagant pensions. Taxpayers (and bond buyers) are increasingly saying "enough."

What might labor relations 2.0 look like? Unions can do more to help workers continually upgrade their skills, and they must work collaboratively with management to improve productivity. Overall, organized labor must adapt to an economy in which jobs involve a more diverse and sophisticated array of tasks and in which employers, both private and public, face relentless pressure to improve efficiency.

Respect the environment as a long-term asset. The environment is our most fundamental asset. We have a moral obligation to pass this asset on to future generations undiminished, or perhaps even improved. Curiously, the same supposed "conservatives" who rightfully lambaste our fiscal policies for the burdens they will pass on to our children and grandchildren are often blithely unconcerned about reckless environmental policies that have the same effect. We are consuming what belongs to the future. In the case of climate change, we are knowingly exposing future generations to significant harms by refusing to make modest changes to our own lifestyles.

Republicans may choose to pretend otherwise, but there is a scientific consensus that man-made climate change is affecting our environment. Furthermore, the debate over climate science is a complete red herring. *As a matter of logic, we do not need conclusive proof that climate change is*

*under way to justify taking action. We need only confirm that
it is a serious potential risk, at which point it would be foolish
not to implement policies to mitigate that risk.*

There is an environmental lesson in the 2008 financial
crisis. The global economic meltdown was brought on by
three fundamental causes: 1) private individuals and firms
acting recklessly; 2) a regulatory structure that was insuf-
ficient to protect the broader system from irresponsible
private actions; and 3) all of us—experts and observers
alike—grossly underestimating the interconnectedness of
the global financial system and the degree to which a handful of financial shocks would set in motion a devastating
chain reaction around the world.

If we think for a moment about our "global ecological
system" rather than the "global financial system," couldn't
all three of those conditions describe our current shortsighted approach to climate change?

Environmental policy is not just about the future. We
live better *today* because of the environmental foresight of
past policymakers. Most policies to protect the environment
impose some economic cost in the short run; to understand
why this trade-off is often worth making, let's look *back-
ward.* Was Teddy Roosevelt foolish to set aside enormous
stretches of land as national parks? Should we repeal the
Clean Air and Clean Water Acts? Should we bring back
leaded gasoline? Isn't it nice that the bald eagle, the sym-
bol of the United States of America, is no longer at risk of
extinction?

Yes, Teddy Roosevelt's national parks were bad news for
real estate developers who might have built condos in what

is now Yellowstone National Park. He destroyed construction jobs! He hurt economic growth! Good for him.

At the same time, we cannot afford to have a theological view of environmental protection. The activities that create comfort and prosperity—such as manufacturing and transportation and heating our homes—will always have some environmental costs. The most logical way to balance growth and environmental responsibility is to build the price of pollution into the activities that cause it. Rational people respond to prices, and rational prices should reflect the true "social cost" of any activity. Coal is not a "cheap" source of energy when its environmental impacts are taken into account.

Pollution taxes, particularly a tax on carbon emissions, would encourage cost-effective conservation; consumers and companies can respond in whatever ways make the most economic sense to them. Any tax on pollution would also make cleaner sources of energy more economically viable. The market is a remarkably powerful phenomenon for creating sane environmental policies—if we give participants the right price signals, which we have failed to do so far.

Build an efficient social safety net. The United States should have a social safety net worthy of the richest society in the history of human civilization—for two reasons. First, it is the humane thing to do, as every major faith throughout history has admonished. It is immoral for humans to be sleeping on sewer grates in a country that can clearly afford to offer something better. One in five American children currently lives in poverty. That is not defensible.

Second, a finely woven safety net provides *political lubrication* for our engine of prosperity by providing meaningful assistance to those who are run over. Everything good about competition creates social costs too. We have built a successful society based on creative destruction. Capitalism is a constant process of breaking things in order to provide something better.

Matthew Slaughter, a Dartmouth economist who worked in the George W. Bush administration, coauthored a seminal article in *Foreign Affairs* providing an intriguing conservative rationale for more redistribution: *give more to the disenfranchised so that they don't kill our golden goose with pitchforks and make us all worse off.* I have obviously put words in his mouth, and the article only addressed the political blowback from trade and globalization. Still, the message has broader social significance. What Slaughter and his coauthor Kenneth Sheve wrote was this: "The notion of more aggressively redistributing income may sound radical, but ensuring that most American workers are benefiting is the best way of saving globalization from a protectionist backlash."[34]

Remember, that is coming from a center-right perspective. The crucial point is that a meaningful safety net will ease the backlash against an inherently disruptive system that often upends lives and communities in the process of doing new and better things.

Of course there is an economic cost associated with any kind of redistribution. The only way to tighten the safety net without busting the budget is to target programs more finely. Government benefits should go to those who really need them.

Before you get too excited about this pearl of wisdom, think about what it means. Some of our most expensive government programs lavish benefits on the middle class, and even on those who are extremely wealthy. That has to change. The affluent should pay more for health care under Medicare and be taxed fully on their Social Security benefits. We must cap or phase out popular but expensive government giveaways that have little or no social value, like the home mortgage-interest deduction. The fact that Bill Gates and Warren Buffett are eligible for a government housing subsidy is indefensible. That is how we achieve smaller, smarter government.

Restore fiscal sanity. We cannot continue to borrow massively from the rest of the world. Our mounting debt is unfair to future generations, leaves the nation dangerously beholden to foreign creditors, and puts the financial system at risk. As we should have learned from our own housing crisis and the Greek debt crisis, when markets lose confidence, the plunge is fast and devastating. When will investors lose confidence in American debt? I have no idea—but we will be caught by surprise when it happens. There is never a memo announcing that a financial crisis will begin in six weeks.

Our overall goal must be to bring the budget back in balance. We must do two crucial things to make that happen:

√   Reform entitlements. We've made promises that
    we cannot afford to keep. According to projections,
    by roughly 2040, three federal programs will con-

sume *all* of federal revenues: Medicaid, Medicare, and Social Security. That does not include defense, education, interest on the debt, *or any other federal spending*. These figures are not political; they are math.

Social Security is relatively straightforward to fix, since we can calculate with some precision what workers will pay into the system and what we will owe to the expected stream of retirees. Over the long run, those numbers need to balance. The most important and obvious reform—which can take us a long way toward restoring solvency to the system—is raising the retirement age to account for the fact that Americans are living much longer than they were when the program was designed. Here, and with all other entitlement programs, the crucial point is that what we pay into the system has to be consistent with what we have promised ourselves we will take out. There are no other short cuts.

√   **Fix health care.** The American health-care system currently consumes 18 percent of GDP, which dwarfs health-care spending in all other developed nations. Worse still, we are not getting great health for all our spending. When the World Health Organization ranked health systems around the globe in 2000, the United States was listed as thirty-seventh, right behind Costa Rica and right ahead of Slovenia.[35] Most Americans believe they are paying a lot for a system that gives them a lot. In fact, we are paying a lot for a system that is mediocre by many important measures.

The United States is the leader in medical innovation, but we have no meaningful mechanisms for determining when and how public health-care dollars can be spent most effectively. The system rewards more treatment, including ever more expensive technology, and not necessarily better outcomes. Rising health-care costs are a huge drag on the private sector and account for the fastest-growing items in the federal budget, in the form of Medicare and Medicaid. Much of what we are spending does not seem to be making us healthier.

The United States needs to change the way medicine is practiced so that the emphasis is on prevention, wellness, and cost-effective treatments. The Obama health-care reforms did not do this. Although there are many potentially sensible ideas tucked in the details of the law, the thrust of the reform was to make an unaffordable system bigger. Meanwhile, the Republicans have no meaningful plan for cost containment at all. Mitt Romney repeatedly vowed to repeal Obamacare on "Day One" of his administration. We never heard much about what would happen on "Day Two"—when he would still have faced an inefficient and unaffordable system, albeit one that no longer promised insurance to all Americans.

The idea that competition among private insur-
ers can be used to drive down public health expenditures is completely untested, has not worked in
the private sector, and has not been embraced
by any serious health economist. Worse still, the
Republicans have strenuously opposed any efforts
to use cost-effectiveness as a criterion for public
health expenditures because this would be the
first step toward "death panels" (Sarah Palin's one
enduring contribution to our national health-care
discussion).

To get our budget back in order, we have to
reform Medicare and Medicaid. And to do that,
we need to reform health care in general, which
would have enormous benefits for the private sector as well. The nasty debate around Obamacare
has proved how hard this will be. Health-care
reform is a policy area where Centrist voices can
add great value. It is also one of the few places
where—with sensible policy changes—we might
actually spend less and get more.

Rebuild our international institutions. We need a
revamped set of international institutions to handle all
of the modern issues that transcend national borders. The
institutions developed after World War II laid the groundwork for decades of prosperity and global cooperation.
Many of those institutions need to be reinvented or rein-
vigorated for twenty-first-century challenges.

The international monetary system negotiated at Bret-

ton Woods near the end of World War II has broken down.
The United Nations has stood effectively mute in the face of
the Iraq War, the Rwandan genocide, the rise of al-Qaeda,
the creation of an Iranian nuclear program, and too many
other international challenges. We have no meaningful
international mechanism for dealing with climate change.
The Kyoto Protocol does not include the United States (the
world's largest per capita carbon emitter), does not place
constraints on India and China (the fastest-growing carbon emitters), and has no real enforcement power over the
countries that are signatories.

The United States will likely never again be the sole
global superpower that it was at the end of the twentieth
century. We cannot afford to be the world's policeman, nor
will ascendant countries like China necessarily tolerate it.
We need a new generation of international organizations
with the capacity and authority to enforce an updated
global rulebook for twenty-first-century issues: terror-
ism, arms trafficking, human trafficking, climate change,
nuclear proliferation, international fisheries, border disputes, human rights violations, and even disputes over sat-
ellites and weapons in outer space. The tools we currently
have for international cooperation around these challenges
are ad hoc, outdated, toothless, or nonexistent.

Neither party has made this a priority. (The Republicans are often hostile to the idea of ceding any authority to
international organizations.) The Centrist Party can offer
leadership as we construct international institutions to deal
with issues for the next fifty years, just as a generation of
thoughtful leaders did after World War II.

The Centrist Process

We must also improve *how we go about governance*—how
we approach problems, how we treat disagreement, even
how we elect our leaders. Americans are not merely fed up
with what politicians do; they are fed up with the entire
political process, particularly the corrosive effect of money
in campaigns. We need to make the whole political process
better:

Be pragmatic. Solve problems. What is the problem we
are trying to address? Why isn't the market fixing it? What
policy or policies would produce a better outcome? What
are the costs of such policies, and who will bear them?
What are reasonable potential compromises that would
give most parties most of what they want? Is this a good
idea—regardless of which political party proposed it?

If you listen to traditional politicians, they typically
focus on ideological inputs rather than quality-of-life out-
puts. Democrats will demand that we spend more money
on social programs or impose new regulations, even in the
face of evidence suggesting that the policies will not work
or that they will create a whole new set of problems or that
the costs will exceed the benefits or that there is a more
efficient way to achieve the same basic end. For Democrats, the first impulse is that the government should just
do *something*. (Hence my favorite public policy aphorism:
"Don't just do something; stand there.")

Republicans cling tenaciously to important principles
such as small government, low taxes, and limited regula-

tion. But they typically make two assumptions at odds with the Centrist approach. First, they assume that these policies are ends in themselves rather than policies that promote positive outcomes such as economic growth and innovation. Second, they simply ignore the fact that undesirable "inputs" such as government spending and regulation can also lead to many positive outcomes—including growth and innovation. Instead of a sane discussion that balances the benefits of government intervention against its costs, we get a theological discussion in which lower taxes and less government are always the right choice. And if low taxes are good, then lower taxes must be even better. But it doesn't work that way. Both logic and basic economics tell us that the point is to find a reasonable balance. Of course, balance is exactly what has been lost in our public discourse.

Talk about trade-offs. The most famous lesson in economics applies to all of public policy: there is no such thing as a free lunch. If there were a policy that made everyone better off without any cost or sacrifice, then presumably Harry Truman would have done it. Or George W. Bush. Or Barack Obama in his first term. Can you envision the following conversation:

Rahm Emanuel (Obama's first chief of staff): "Mr. President, our policy wonks in the basement of the Executive Office Building have come up with a set of solutions to balance the federal budget that are good for the economy in both the short and the long run."

President Obama: "What's the bad news?"

Rahm Emanuel: "There is none. Our polling shows

that 100 percent of Americans will heartily support these policies."

President Obama: "Well, I'm very busy with other things. Let's hold off for now."

These discussions do not happen. Instead, we are generally left with four kinds of difficult public choices:

1. *We can make ourselves better off now by sacrificing the future.* As a car salesman might say, "This is our most popular model!" There are times when this makes sense, such as building a highway and paying off the construction bonds over time. But often we are just borrowing marshmallows from the future and gobbling them up without much regard for whoever has to pay back the debt. In any event, the trade-off is clear: live better today by living less well tomorrow.

2. *We can do the opposite: make ourselves better off in the long run with some collective sacrifice in the short run.* We can slow the rate of climate change by raising the costs of current activities that cause carbon pollution, such as burning fossil fuels. That will in turn raise the cost of everything from commuting to work to buying Chilean strawberries at the supermarket. There is a robust discussion that we should have around such a trade-off.

3. *We can do something that makes us all better off in the present—but there are still costs, sacrifices, or some other "side effects."* We can reduce health-care costs by limiting expensive medical procedures that are unproven or produce small improvements in health relative to their costs (such as intensive end-of-life care). We will pay less and get fewer options—like in Canada or Great Britain or just about every other industrialized country. That is the unavoidable trade-off. Of course, the moment this uncomfortable reality was broached in the health-care discussion, it immediately took on the moniker "death panels." The reality is that making health care more affordable (or even slowing the rate of growth in spending) will require fundamental changes in the way medicine is practiced, some of which we will not like. To repeat, we cannot get something for nothing—or we would have chosen that option already.

4. *We can do something that makes most of us better off while imposing significant pain on some small but well-organized and vocal group.* Most farm subsidies do not make any sense for the country as a whole. They *do* put a lot of money in the pockets of American farmers—who are motivated and mobilized to protect their government handouts. Ditto for most of the loopholes in the corporate tax code and the earmarks slipped into our federal transportation bills. The general public would be better off without this buffet of bad policies served up for special interests, but facing down the motivated and organized groups who benefit from them is a Herculean political task. I do not use this metaphor lightly. Cleaning up the tax code is often compared to cleaning out the Aegean stables. (Lots of crap has been piling up for a long time.) When reforms are discussed, the potential losers scream loudly; the rest of us—the potential beneficiaries—do very little singing. Rational politicians respond to what they hear.

Many complex policies, such as health care and education, involve all of these trade-offs. The Centrists are not going to ride in on white horses with miracle cures tucked in the saddle, *because there are no miracle cures.* But there are lots of options that are better than what we are doing now, and those better policies begin with a more sophisticated discussion around the issues. The Centrist Party will facilitate those discussions.

Improve the electoral system. The goals of a representative democracy are fairly basic: 1) elect representatives who reflect the will of their constituents; and 2) provide a forum in which those elected representatives can agree on policies that are in the best long-term interests of the citizens whom they represent.

We need to set about repairing the system. None of the necessary institutional changes will be easy. Those who are in power make rules to protect themselves. The Centrist Party must work steadily on many fronts to improve the overall electoral process so that fewer Americans feel disenfranchised by the system:

Curtail the gerrymandering of congressional districts. There are a number of options for limiting the most egregious abuses of the redistricting process, such as having independent redistricting commissions or even computers create the legislative districts.

Promote open primaries in which the top two candidates in a single primary election advance to the general election, regardless of their political party. (Thus, two Democrats could face one another, or two Republicans.) California has now adopted this system. Candidates no longer need to placate the most extreme members of their own party in order to get on the general election ballot.

Reform the rules in Congress, particularly the Senate, so that one or two intransigent members cannot consistently stand in the way of getting important things done. Each chamber makes its own rules; they can change them. Filibuster reform would be a good start.

Constrain the corrosive effect of money in politics. The Supreme Court has not made this easy, but there is still room to limit the degree to which massively expensive campaigns diminish our faith in the electoral process and discourage good people from running. We can get tougher on donor disclosure. We can be more creative with public financing. We can urge voluntary spending limits.

Ask always, Where are we trying to go? What is a reasonably good way to get there? What do we want society to look like in twenty years? What are measurable outcomes in that regard? We should ask these questions of ourselves. This is not to suggest that government is scientific, or that policymakers should be bloodless technocrats who can make any important decision as long as they have a calculator and scratch paper. It does mean that thoughtfulness and pragmatism should suffuse what government does. We are far more likely to get to a better place as a society if we have thought systematically about what "a better place" might look like.

THE CENTRIST APPROACH—the principles, the goals, the procedural reforms—lays out a path forward for a country whose enormous potential has been waylaid by a broken political system. Are lots of people going to like everything included here? Of course not.

Are these ideas better than what either the Republicans or Democrats are offering? Yes.

Would they help solve some of our nation's most serious challenges? Yes.

And most important for purposes of building a new, credible political party: Is this a reasonable set of beliefs around which pragmatic people could organize? Yes.

So let's do that.

CHAPTER 5

Sex and Guns

Any serious talk of pragmatism and compromise in American politics usually ends with some nettlesome questions: What about the social issues? What about abortion? What about gun control? These are issues on which reasonable people disagree passionately. Anyone who tells you that there is a "right" answer on abortion has not spent much time thinking about the issue, or lacks the empathy to appreciate how other people think about it. Americans' views on these issues tend to be theological—literally in many cases. No amount of arguing or data gathering is going to change anyone's core values; we've dug our intellectual trenches and hunkered down.

So how can a party built around the idea of pragmatism and compromise deal with issues whose defining feature is a deep and conflicting vision of what is right and wrong?

With pragmatism and compromise. Here is the fundamental insight: reasonable people disagree about whether
or not abortion should be illegal; *but no reasonable person
thinks that abortion is a good thing.*

Reasonable people disagree about how readily guns
should be available and what the requirements for pur-
chase ought to be; *but no reasonable person wants guns to
fall into the hands of criminals or those who are dangerously
mentally ill.*

There are plenty of other social issues: drug policy, stem
cell research, flag burning, the death penalty, and so on. In
time, the Centrist Party will have to wrestle with them all.
For now, abortion and guns will do a fine job of illustrat-
ing how the Centrist Party can bring people together on
issues that normally drive them apart. The key to diffusing
these ideologically charged social issues is refocusing them
on two more pragmatic questions: 1) What is the real harm
to society associated with this activity? 2) How can we minimize that harm? The answers to those questions will dic-
tate Centrist policy. Is that going to make everybody happy?
Of course not. But the purpose of the Centrist Party is not
to make everybody happy, particularly the political poles.
The purpose of the Centrist Party is to craft an agenda
that a large swathe of underrepresented moderate American voters can get behind. On the major social issues, that's
entirely possible.

Let me pause to note that there is one prominent issue
missing from that introduction: gay marriage. The Centrist Party must support gay marriage for the simple reason that there is no legitimate reason to be against it. What

is the potential harm to society associated with same-sex marriage? Answer: *there is none.* Marriage is a private contract between two consenting adults. It is the capstone to a loving relationship that also bestows significant legal rights. There must be some compelling harm that spills over to the rest of society if government is to stand in the way of this private behavior. But there is not. How might it be bad *for society in general* if two people of the same sex decide to enter into a legal relationship? As a former military officer once grumbled to me, "I don't have to like it. I just don't think it's any of my business." The notion that gay marriage somehow diminishes heterosexual marriage would be laugh-out-loud funny if it were not the most common rationalization for denying gay couples a basic right.

The Centrist Party will support gay marriage because it is consistent with the Centrist principles (chapter 4: "When private behavior does not affect the rest of us, then we ought to let individuals decide what is appropriate and what is not"). This is a position, by the way, that both liberals and small-government conservatives ought to agree on. Gay marriage promotes social justice (a traditional liberal objective) by granting new rights to a group that has historically been discriminated against. It also gets government out of the business of arbitrating private morality (a traditional conservative objective). Obviously there is a significant clash on this issue between traditional conservatives, who favor small government with a limited reach, and social conservatives, who are eager to have government police private behavior. This is only one of many areas in which the core constituencies of the Republican Party are fundamentally at odds with one another.

For the Centrists, there is no need to compromise on this issue because there is no intellectually legitimate difference of opinion. As an aside, supporting gay marriage is also good politics in the long run. A Gallup poll conducted in 2011 found that for the first time a majority of Americans support gay marriage (53 percent), up from only 27 percent in 1996.[36] In twenty years, this won't be a mainstream issue. In a private conversation, a senior Gallup official said that he has never seen a social issue on which opinions have changed so quickly. Not only are attitudes changing fast, but young Americans are far more likely to support gay marriage than older Americans. The same Gallup poll found that 70 percent of eighteen- to thirty-four-year-olds support gay marriage, compared to only 39 percent of those fifty-five and older. Young people will get older; old people will die. Even if no single American changes his or her mind on this issue, the passage of time alone will lead to a steady change in overall public opinion, assuming young generations continue to be more comfortable with homosexuality than older generations.

Gay marriage is an anomaly among social issues in that the argument is so intellectually lopsided. Abortion and gun control, along with most social issues, involve legitimate ideological differences that are irreconcilable. Both sides have defensible views (as much as their opponents would like to pretend otherwise). Still, there is a political path forward.

Abortion

Let's start with abortion. Anyone who has been in America for longer than six months is familiar with the competing narratives. If one believes that life begins at conception, then every abortion stops a beating heart. For those who view abortion as akin to murder, society has an obligation to protect the innocent unborn. The belief that life begins at conception is entirely defensible, and if one believes that, then of course abortion ought to be illegal—for the same reason that it is illegal to kill a two-year-old.

The obvious countervailing view is that society has no right to tell a woman what to do with her body. A developing fetus is inextricably linked to the woman carrying it; government ought not compel her to carry and deliver a baby against her will. If one believes that the rights of a pregnant woman trump those of her unborn baby, then abortion should be legal. This, too, is a defensible position.

And so, the issue is seemingly irreconcilable, with roughly half of Americans describing themselves as pro-choice and about the same proportion describing themselves as pro-life. Abortion is the epitome of political trench warfare. America's abortion policies have not changed fundamentally since the Supreme Court decided the *Roe v. Wade* case, yet we fight skirmish after skirmish on the margins (waiting periods, mandatory vaginal ultrasounds, etc.). The most serious problem for the country is that the abortion issue contaminates every other facet of politics and governance: every election, every judicial appointment, every discussion around public funding for women's health. The philosophical disagreements over abortion policy may be defensible, but the degree to which that single issue paralyzes the nation on other issues is not. We need to move forward.

The pragmatic way to move forward is to seize on two areas around this contentious issue where most Americans are more likely to agree than disagree. First, most Americans are more ambivalent in their views about abortion than the polls might first suggest. Once one moves away from the political extremes, the chasm between pro-choice and pro-life grows more ambiguous. Two thought exercises will help illuminate this point.

Thought exercise number 1: If you are pro-life, then presumably you believe that a fetus deserves government protection. According to this worldview, a developing fetus is a person, and killing a person is not a "choice." Okay, fair enough.

Yet, if you are pro-life, there is a good chance that you also believe that exceptions ought to be made in the cases of rape and incest. According to Gallup, only a small minority of Americans believe that abortion should be illegal in all circumstances; rape and incest are typically offered as exceptions.[37]

The curious thing about this seemingly reasonable position is that it has a fundamental inconsistency. Would you allow a woman to terminate the life of a two-year-old who was born of rape or incest? Probably not. If a fetus deserves the same protection as a two-year-old, why does the source of conception make any difference at all? It doesn't. Instead, the Americans who believe that abortion should be illegal except for cases of rape and incest are really thinking about the mother; *a woman should not be forced to carry a baby against her will in some circumstances.* There is a glimmer of pro-choice thinking there, and that ought to give us some hope for building a Centrist consensus on this issue.

Now for thought exercise number 2: If you are pro-choice, here are some questions for you. Does it make you uncomfortable if a woman uses abortion as a form of birth control? Does it make you uncomfortable when families in China and India use abortion to select the sex of their child? Do you feel less comfortable with legal abortion in the second or third trimester than in the first? Would you support a woman who decided to abort a fetus with brown eyes because she preferred a blue-eyed baby (or some other genetic endowment)? If you answered yes to some or all of these questions, then you resemble many Americans who describe themselves as pro-choice. Again according to Gallup, only a fifth of Americans believe abortion should be legal in all circumstances.

And no one is pro-abortion. Very few pro-choice Americans really believe that having an abortion is the moral equivalent of having an appendix removed. A high proportion of pro-choice voters would defend a woman's right to terminate a pregnancy while still describing every abortion as a mistake, a tragedy, or both.

Building on all of this, the Centrist Party can cobble together a consensus around a policy that advocates for the following: 1) Safe and legal access to abortion (and widespread availability of products caught up in the abortion debate, such as the "morning-after pill"). 2) A concerted effort to reduce the number of abortions, including greater access to contraceptives, comprehensive sex education, and a better social safety net for poor women. (One of the most common stated reasons for getting an abortion is a financial inability to have and raise the child.) 3) Placement of some limits on abortion services *provided that they are not designed exclusively to curtail access to abortion or to humiliate women.* If, for example, evidence suggests that a significant number of women choose not to have an abortion when some mandatory waiting period is put in place—*a genuine change of heart*—then it would be perfectly reasonable to mandate such a waiting period. This is consistent with the goal of providing safe access to abortion while also minimizing the number of abortions. However, if evidence suggests that the effect of a waiting period is merely to erect a barrier to a legal medical procedure, particularly for low-income women, then there is no place for it.

This kind of non-absolutist policy is consistent with what most Americans say they want. Most important, this is a policy around which a wide swath of moderate voters can rally, particularly the growing number of young voters who describe themselves as "fiscally conservative and socially liberal." We can get beyond the trench warfare of abortion politics, for a number of reasons. First, the Centrist policy outlined here is largely consistent with the status quo. Centrist candidates would not be crusading to make radical changes on this issue; they can spend their time and effort focusing on the many important American challenges beyond abortion.

Second, the Centrist Party will acknowledge the legitimacy of the pro-life viewpoint and seek to deliver what those Americans ostensibly care most about: fewer abortions. To do that, we will have to get past many of the most counterproductive policies of the pro-life movement. We should not pretend that abstinence education is sufficient to prevent unwanted pregnancies among teens. Both common sense and extensive research suggest that abstinence education alone does not work.

We should not cut off government funding for women's health centers that provide abortion services. These clinics typically provide other important health services, including ones that are crucial to preventing unwanted pregnancies, such as access to contraceptives. Meanwhile, we should provide access to contraception and sex education in the United States and around the world. (Most abortions take place in the developing world.)

Finally, the Centrist position on abortion is pragmatic. Social conservatives are fighting a symbolic but losing battle. Abortion is never going to be illegal in most of America; focusing on that objective is a fool's errand. Let's think about what it would take to outlaw abortion. The first step would be overturning the *Roe v. Wade* decision. A conservative president might appoint a Supreme Court justice willing to do that, and the new justice might find four other votes. However, one of the important pillars of constitutional law is respect for precedent, which makes overturning *Roe* less likely with each passing year.

Still, it could happen. Overturning *Roe* would not make abortion illegal, however; it would merely open the door for the states to do so. (Even before the *Roe v. Wade* decision, there was no federal ban on abortion, and it is profoundly unlikely that Congress would ever pass such a ban.) In a post-*Roe* world, abortion would still be legal in many states. Abortions would also be performed illegally (and often unsafely) in states that criminalized the procedure. All of which brings us to the most salient fact underlying the Centrist position on this issue: *the abortion rate is shockingly invariant to whether abortion is legal or not.* According to a study in the British medical journal *Lancet*, countries with restrictive abortion laws do not have lower rates of abortion.[38] *Western Europe, where abortion is legal and widely available, has an abortion rate that is 43 percent lower than the rate in the United States.*

Contemplate this: Has the United States ever convened a serious, high-profile nonpartisan commission, with representation from across the abortion ideological spectrum, to recommend policies that would bring the abortion rate down, apart from making the procedure illegal? No, because we cannot get past the legality debate, even though it is essentially symbolic at this point. The pro-life movement has been consumed with making noise rather than making a difference. As a result, we have roughly twice the abortion rate of countries that have taken a more pragmatic approach. *That is a tragedy with no political winner.*

So let's summarize what the Centrist Party can offer as an alternative to the current abortion trench warfare: a policy that respects women's rights, acknowledges the legitimacy of pro-life views, reduces the number of unintended pregnancies, lowers the abortion rate, minimizes government involvement in private medical decisions, and moves abortion politics to the back burner—all without overturning a forty-year-old Supreme Court precedent or changing any major federal laws. A very large number of American voters can get behind that policy.

Guns

Americans love their guns. And by "Americans," I mean both law-abiding citizens using guns for recreation and self-defense and the criminals who use guns to commit 11,500 murders every year.[39] The Centrist approach is straightforward: respect the gun rights of the former while doing everything possible to keep weapons out of the hands of the latter. There is no inherent conflict between those two objectives.

Proponents of gun rights believe they have a constitutional right to bear arms: for hunting, for self-defense, for whatever else strikes them. The Second Amendment may be one of the sloppier pieces of writing done by our Founding Fathers, but the Supreme Court has affirmed and clarified the right to bear arms. We are not taking away America's guns anytime soon.

Gun control advocates, particularly those who live in and around urban areas, believe that restraints on gun ownership would save lives. Among developed countries, the United States is a uniquely violent place, and guns play a role in making that violence deadly. Every kind of criminal activity, from drug dealing to domestic violence, is made worse when guns are involved.

Let's give everyone most of what they want. Taking guns out of the hands of gang bangers in Chicago would

not impinge in any significant way on the life of someone
who likes to hunt deer in Wisconsin, or on someone in Washington, D.C., who wants to keep a gun in the house for self-
defense (which is a right that the Supreme Court recently
affirmed). We can reduce the number of gun crimes, accom-
modate a full range of hunting and other gun-related recre-
ational activities, and allow responsible people to own guns
in their homes. It just requires a modicum of common sense.

The key to making guns less dangerous is focusing on the
mechanism by which guns get into the hands of criminals.
Guns are different from drugs such as cocaine and meth-
amphetamine. Guns cannot be manufactured in makeshift
labs in the jungle, or by high school dropouts in basements
and garages. The guns that kill innocent victims on our
streets come off a legal assembly line, just like cars and televisions. Most are sold legally at retail stores or gun shows,
also like cars and televisions. And then sometime after that,
they fall into the hands of thugs and psychopaths who have
a vicious disregard for human life. The Centrist strategy
has one overriding focus: intercept the flow of guns moving
from the right hands into the wrong hands.

Doing that requires two broad steps. First, the Centrist
Party must unequivocally support the rights of law-abiding
Americans to own and use guns, including handguns, for
recreation and self-defense. This position is consistent with
the most recent Supreme Court interpretation of the Second Amendment. It is also a position that is acceptable to
most political moderates. (Your decision to keep a gun under
your pillow is your business.) Most important, it undercuts
the disingenuous (but highly effective) argument of the

National Rifle Association (NRA) and other gun zealots
that placing any constraints on gun ownership is merely
the first step in a plot to ban all guns for all people.

Second, the Centrist Party must demand the same
responsibility from gun owners that we expect from anyone
else handling a potentially dangerous product. Car owners
must register their vehicles. Pharmacists must account
for opiates and other addictive drugs in their possession.
Defense contractors must ensure that secret technologies
do not fall into the hands of hostile governments. The idea
that gun owners can buy, sell, and use lethal weapons without any government oversight is delusional.

In fact, let's put the gun carnage in perspective. Roughly
three thousand Americans died in the terrorist attacks that
happened on September 11, 2001. Ever since, we have
been expending enormous resources and impinging on the
rights of law-abiding citizens to prevent any such attacks
in the future. Most of us are okay with the majority of the
antiterrorism measures that have been put in place. *All the
while, every year guns are killing nearly four times as many
Americans as the 9/11 attacks did.* We should do something
about that.

And here is what we should do: Every owner of a gun—
from the factory producing firearms to the guy putting a
pistol under his pillow at night—must be responsible for
every weapon in his or her possession. More specifically,
every new gun produced in the United States or imported
from abroad must be licensed. When a weapon changes
hands legally, from retailer to owner, or from private owner
to private owner, the license for that particular weapon

must accompany the transaction, just like a car title changes hands at the point of sale. Anyone with a legal weapon will have "title" to it. That title will lay out the history of the weapon—every owner since it came off the assembly line. For weapons already in circulation, there would be some transition period, say six months, during which existing gun owners would be required to license their weapons. After that, owning an unlicensed weapon becomes a crime. *Because if law-abiding citizens are going to exercise their constitutional right to bear arms, they have an obligation to society to do it in a safe and responsible way.*

Technology has the potential to turn gun licensing from an annoying bureaucratic hurdle into a powerful tool for keeping guns out of the wrong hands (or figuring out how they got there). One possible example: each licensed weapon could have a "ballistic fingerprint" that is registered with the federal government at the time of manufacture, or when an existing weapon is licensed for the first time. The ballistic fingerprint is the unique mark that a gun barrel imparts on a bullet when fired. (This is the same science that law enforcement has been using for decades to determine if a bullet found at a crime scene was fired from a particular weapon.) A gun's identifying ballistic pattern is much harder to erase or file away than a serial number. The result is that every legal firearm would be licensed to a specific owner and a have a unique fingerprint. If a licensed gun is lost or stolen, the owner has an obligation to report the loss to law enforcement authorities.

Is this a hassle for gun owners? Of course it is. So is waiting in line at the Department of Motor Vehicles to get a driver's license. That is the price that comes with owning and operating a product that has the potential, when mishandled, to kill or injure other members of society.

What would we get for that hassle? The "fingerprint and license" system enables us to answer the most important question when a particular gun (or a bullet fired from a particular gun) turns up at a crime scene: Where did this gun come from?

This kind of plan moves beyond the questions that gun control advocates usually ask: Who needs to buy twenty handguns? Or, should we ban semiautomatic weapons? Those are the wrong questions. They are all about constraining the rights of law-abiding citizens. Here is the right question: After you bought twenty handguns, why and how did eighteen of them end up in the hands of gang members on the streets of Detroit?

If your gun—one of the twenty handguns you purchased last month—is used in a crime and you have not reported it lost or stolen, then you have some questions to answer. And if your "lost" guns repeatedly turn up in the wrong hands, then perhaps you should spend some time in prison, or on the receiving end of a civil lawsuit.

This policy is no panacea for gun violence. It's a patch, not a cure. The cure is eliminating the gangs, the domestic violence, the drug trade, and so on. Gun advocates have always been right about that. Nor will licensing and fingerprinting necessarily stop the random mass killings in schools and theaters, because the weapons involved in those massacres are often purchased legally by people who have not yet manifested signs that they are dangerous or mentally ill.

This policy also skirts the contentious issue of concealed weapons. If you have a gun in your home, then it is essentially your business. But when you take that gun to work or to the supermarket, then it becomes everyone's business. Americans are divided about the right to carry concealed weapons. There is no obvious policy compromise, at least not at the federal level. The Centrist approach to this divisive debate would be to lean on federalism. States can decide their own concealed carry laws, contingent upon those guns being licensed as described earlier. It doesn't much matter in Massachusetts if people are taking guns to the mall in Texas, *provided that those guns are licensed, "fingerprinted," and don't somehow end up in the hands of a Boston street gang.*

A pragmatic licensing policy would help keep guns out of the hands of violent people (and introduce some accountability when guns do end up in the wrong places). True, there are so many guns already in the wrong hands that criminals will still have access to illicit weapons. But it is disingenuous to argue that we should not keep better track of weapons in the future because we have done such a poor job of keeping track of them in the past. Licensing and fingerprinting would raise the street price of illegal guns, perhaps keeping more of them out of the hands of street punks. When guns do end up in the wrong hands, we would have another tool for figuring out how it happened.

On the political front, any sane gun policy runs square into the logical fallacies of the NRA, which has promulgated the myth that any restriction on gun rights leads to a "slippery slope" in which all gun rights will be whittled away: if we as a society make it harder for gang bangers to buy twenty guns in Missouri, then soon it will be illegal to hunt deer in Wisconsin. This belief violates both common sense and formal logic. At the risk of becoming overly pedantic, there is no such thing as a slippery slope. If you believe that owning a bazooka is a bad thing, but deer hunting with a rifle seems perfectly sensible, then we can vote to ban bazookas without eliminating deer hunting. The political logic of groups like the NRA is that even the most benign and sensible restrictions on gun owners merely empower the anti-gun forces to ask for less benign and less sensible restrictions.

But why? Most Americans have no problem with hunting or keeping guns in the home. The fact is that gun owners can have everything they want in exchange for exercising a modicum of responsibility with a lethal weapon. The NRA stands in the path of that "modicum of responsibility." The Centrist Party is about wrestling the country away from extremist groups whose views are out of sync with those of most Americans. And behold, the policy I have described is something that most moderate voters could live with. The Centrist gun policy unequivocally supports the rights of law-abiding Americans to have and use guns; it demands responsibility from gun manufacturers, retailers, and owners; and it uses technology to keep weapons out of the wrong hands.

Isn't that better than what we've been doing?

MORE BROADLY, ISN'T the Centrist approach to social issues a refreshing change to the overheated Democratic and Republican rhetoric? This is an important part of the

Centrist Party appeal. On issues like gay marriage and abortion, the Centrists will respect individual rights in ways that are traditionally considered liberal and have therefore been the domain of the Democrats. But this approach to social issues will no longer be tethered to the Democrats' muddled thinking on economic issues. The result is a combination that describes many moderate voters, particularly young voters: "socially liberal and fiscally conservative."

The combination of sensible economic policies and a progressive approach to social issues will peel voters away from both parties. From the Republicans, the Centrist Party will dislodge the economic conservatives who have zero interest in the right-wing social agenda but cannot bring themselves to support the Democrats' populist and undisciplined approach to taxes, regulation, and fiscal policy.

From the Democrats, the Centrist Party will dislodge the voters who respect small government and fiscal responsibility but cannot bring themselves to support the Republicans' heavy-handed, right-wing social agenda.

Pragmatic moderates will no longer have to tolerate the crazies in their own party because they consider them to be less scary or offensive than the crazies in the other party. Far from being a collection of insolvable stumbling blocks, social issues have the potential to be a defining strength of the Centrist Party.

CHAPTER 6

Making It Happen:
The Centrist Strategy

THE Republicans and the Democrats are institutionally entrenched. Americans have their minds wrapped around a two-party system. It is hard to get people to envision something different—despite the fact that there have been tectonic changes in the American political parties at many different junctures in our history. Building a new political party from scratch feels daunting and naïve.

But look at Google, or Amazon.com, or the iPhone. Americans are brilliant innovators—in the private sector. We worship entrepreneurs. We are constantly looking for ways to do everything better. So why would we tolerate two outdated political parties stuck in a broken system, decade after decade?

What we are talking about here is political innovation. We are offering a political party that would be better for many American voters than the choices they have now. *A lot better.*

The quirky nature of the American federal system makes all of this possible. As noted earlier, the Centrist strategy begins by capturing a handful of U.S. Senate seats, presumably in New England, the Midwest, or any number of swing states. Angus King was elected to the Senate from Maine in 2012 as a moderate independent. Consider him Centrist number one. Senator King will caucus with the Democrats, but he has stated that he hopes to be a bipartisan bridge builder. We need to give Angus some more Centrist buddies in the Senate.

Once the Centrists control four or five U.S. Senate seats, the party will hold the swing votes necessary for either the Republicans or the Democrats (including the president) to do *anything.** The Centrists would be the gatekeepers for the entire federal government. But unlike the Tea Party extremists, or the obstructionist parties that hold their governments hostage in parliamentary systems elsewhere in the world, the Centrist Party would not be making demands that are out of sync with mainstream American public opinion. The Centrists would be a small, disproportionately powerful bloc demanding what most Americans are asking for. The Centrist Party could use its fulcrum of power in the U.S. Senate to force Republi-

---

* Even if the Senate were more lopsided, say, fifty-eight Democrats, three Centrists, and thirty-nine Republicans, the Centrist votes would determine whether the minority party could filibuster or not.

cans and Democrats to come to sensible compromises on important issues.

To recap: 1) Centrist candidates need to win only 34 percent of the vote in three or four more U.S. Senate races (if we count Angus King as number one). 2) If the Centrists can deny either party a majority in the U.S. Senate, then the Centrist Party would hold the swing votes necessary to get anything done. 3) Having exploited this quirk in the American structure, the Centrists can steer the country in a sane, pragmatic direction that promotes long-term strength, security, and prosperity. This plan is entirely feasible, particularly if young, pragmatic leaders from around the country are willing to get behind it.

Still, let's dispense with the skeptics. Yes, the American political system has historically been hostile to third parties. Any serious political observer knows that. We have had many third-party presidential candidates, from Teddy Roosevelt of the Bull Moose Party to Ralph Nader of the Green Party. They don't win. And to the extent that they change the political landscape, it is often in ways that distort voters' preferences. Ralph Nader arguably made George W. Bush president in 2000 by taking votes away from Al Gore in Florida. That's hardly what Nader supporters could have hoped for.

Even if a third-party presidential candidate were to catch fire with voters—perhaps even winning a plurality of votes cast—the Electoral College is more hostile still. The outcome of a close presidential race would be decided by the House of Representatives. Since no third party is likely to have a majority of votes in the House, the presi-

dential bid would end there. Americans like to focus their
political attention on the White House, but the presidency
is a dead end in terms of transforming the current political
landscape.

The House of Representatives is not much better. Both
the Democrats and the Republicans can and would use
their redistricting power to draw congressional districts
that squelch any incipient Centrist movement. So forget
the House of Representatives too.

The Centrist strategy has to be built around the U.S.
Senate. Imagine a Senate that has forty-seven Republicans,
forty-nine Democrats, and four Centrists. As noted earlier,
neither party can do anything in this scenario without the
cooperation of the Centrists. And nothing can happen in
the federal government without the Senate. *This is a quirk
in the American system that has never been exploited.* A third
party with a handful of seats in the Senate would essentially run the country.

Our Centrist Nation

Electing four Centrist senators would not be fabulously
difficult. Neither the Democrats nor the Republicans can
gerrymander a Senate race. The state is the "district," and
everyone in the state can vote. There are plenty of states
that consistently elect Democrats and Republicans to statewide office, making a Centrist candidate who combines the
best of each party a very attractive candidate.

Any state in New England could elect a Centrist senator
(or another Centrist, if we consider Angus King the first).

New England used to be the home of the moderate wing of the Republican Party, back before moderate Republicans were put on the endangered species list. Those politicians and the voters who supported that wing of the party would now be most comfortable as Centrists.

In Maine, Angus King replaced Olympia Snowe, the moderate Republican who served three terms in the Senate before leaving in exasperation over the growing partisanship. In a reformed system, Olympia Snowe might have been a Centrist. So might her fellow senator from Maine, Susan Collins, who also has a reputation for joining with Democrats to find common ground.

Lincoln Chafee was a moderate Republican senator from Rhode Island until he became so fed up with the party that he quit and became an independent. Rhode Island voters then elected him governor.

There are twelve potential Centrist Senate seats just in New England.

The Midwest states also tend to elect both Republicans and Democrats. My former home state of Illinois is represented in the Senate by Dick Durbin, a Democrat, and Mark Kirk, a Republican. One curious feature of Illinois politics is that the last two governors have gone to jail. The good news for the Centrists is that one was a Republican and the other was a Democrat. Illinois could easily send a Centrist to prison, or to the Senate.

Iowa, Wisconsin, Minnesota, and Ohio all have the same tendency to elect both Republicans and Democrats.

The Midwest: at least another ten potential Senate seats.

Then there are the states that have emerged as "swing

states" in recent presidential elections: Virginia, Pennsylvania, Florida, Nevada, Colorado. By definition, a swing state has a large contingent of voters who might vote for a Republican or for a Democrat in any given year. The right candidate in any of those swing states could win as a Centrist.

Swing states: another ten potential Senate seats. Plus California and a few other states that vote consistently Republican or Democrat in the presidential election but still occasionally elect a governor or senator from the other party (e.g., Arnold Schwarzenegger as a Republican governor in California and Brian Schweitzer as a Democratic governor in Montana).

None of this should be shocking; *remember, the largest and fastest-growing bloc of voters are those who do not identify themselves as Democrats or Republicans.* These non-aligned voters are tipping elections one way or the other. A Centrist candidate running statewide is likely to offer what this broad spectrum of the electorate is looking for. But it is even better than that. A Centrist candidate does not have to talk crazy during the primary. He or she can address important issues in a sensible way *from the very beginning of the election.* Even if multiple Centrist candidates were competing for the nomination, they would all be seeking support in the political middle, not on the tails.

This is a crucial point. Let's drill down further on how a U.S. Senate race in any of these states would likely play out. A typical Senate race begins with each major party selecting its candidate in a primary election. As in any primary, the strategy for both Republicans and Democrats is to

appeal to the "base." In some states, only registered Republicans or Democrats can vote in their respective primaries.
In all states, the primaries attract the most committed and
partisan members of each party.

Both Republican and Democratic candidates say and do
things during the primary that are designed to energize the
most polarized elements of their parties. You have watched
this movie. The primaries are about political crazy talk,
much of which typically ends when each party has a nominee. The winning candidates subsequently rush toward
the political center as they face off in the general election.
The Mitt Romney presidential campaign contributed the
term "etch-a-sketch" to our political lexicon when a campaign aide described the process by which Romney would
erase the extreme positions he took during the primaries
and write new positions as he began courting swing voters
in the general election. Romney was merely doing what
every Republican and Democratic candidate tries to do in a
general election. Most of the pandering to the base has to
be jettisoned because moderate voters—the ones who will
determine the winner—are repulsed by it.

This whole dynamic is a gift to Centrist candidates.
When the Republican and Democratic candidates win
their respective primaries and rush back to the political
center, *that space on the spectrum will already be taken.* The
Centrist candidate will have been talking for months about
issues that resonate with general election voters.

And remember: any candidate, including a Centrist,
need only capture a plurality of the votes cast to win a
U.S. Senate race. The candidate with the most votes wins,

regardless of whether that candidate gets a majority or not. As noted earlier, this is crucial to the whole strategy: a Centrist candidate can win a Senate seat with as little as 34 percent of the vote.

There is nothing naïve about thinking that a Centrist candidate can win 34 percent of the vote in a handful of states, particularly when the Republican and Democratic candidates are disadvantaged in the general election by the things they have to say and do to win their respective primaries.

All of that brings us to the political scenario described earlier: a Senate with forty-nine Democrats, forty-seven Republicans, and four Centrists (or some split along those lines). Those Centrist senators now wield the power to determine what passes in Congress, and what does not.

A handful of Centrists can have two enormous positive impacts in terms of breaking the current Washington gridlock. First and most obvious, these Centrist senators will be legislative power brokers. To be politically feasible, any piece of legislation would have to appeal to the political middle that the Centrists represent. The Republicans would have to adapt their proposals to pick up Centrist votes, as would the Democrats.

Meanwhile, the Centrist Party has the potential to be the intellectual home for sensible proposals on a broad range of issues. Just as the bipartisan Simpson-Bowles commission proposed a series of fiscal suggestions that were widely embraced by policy experts, the Centrist Party could be a repository of similar thinking on other issues—a permanent Simpson-Bowles process. Since any proposal is a nonstarter without Centrist support, the logical question would become, "What's the Centrist position on this?" The Centrist Party should have an arsenal of good answers to that question. In an earlier era, this is what bipartisan groups of Republicans and Democrats used to do. The Centrist Party would become an institutional fix for the breakdown of bipartisanship.

To succeed at all this, the Centrist Party must bring national money and organization to bear on the Senate races where there is the most hope of winning. The first step is to pick the particular states where Centrist candidates will do well in a particular election. There may be an open seat, or an attractive Centrist candidate, or a high-profile Republican or Democrat willing to defect to the Centrist Party. Step one of the national strategy is to identify those most promising races and candidates.

Step two is to mobilize the nation's frustrated moderates behind the Centrist candidates in those targeted races. The key to making that happen—to getting on the ballot and running a solid, well-financed candidate—is putting fifty states' worth of money and organizational muscle behind those handpicked Senate races. Any Centrist candidate is going to face formidable Republican and Democratic organizations. The two parties are going to fight not only to win the seat, but to nip the potent Centrist challenge in the bud.

To counter that, imagine harnessing deep pockets across the country—not the usual partisan types, but the pragmatic civic leaders who are deeply worried about our nation's problems and Washington's inability to deal with them. Recent changes in campaign finance laws make it extremely easy to direct national resources to statewide races. Ironically, this broken feature of the current electoral system can be turned to the Centrists' advantage (until we get it fixed). A Centrist super PAC (political action committee) can drop tens of millions of dollars collected around the country into a Senate race in Rhode Island, New Hampshire, Illinois, or anywhere else that augurs well for a pathbreaking Centrist candidate.

The first few Senate elections will be expensive, brutal slogs. Still, a national Centrist Party, mobilizing an entire country of moderate voters fed up with the current gridlock, can beat back the stale political status quo. In the long run, Centrist success will breed additional success in two important ways.

First, the Centrist momentum will feed on itself. The Centrist Party will attract independent voters and the most pragmatic, moderate voters from each of the two traditional parties. As that happens, both the Democrats and the Republicans will drift farther left and right, respectively. Each party will be more radical than it was before the creation of the Centrist Party.

As the Republicans move right and the Democrats move left, some of the moderates remaining in each party will feel less comfortable. (Imagine yourself as a moderate Republican who suddenly finds herself in the Tea Party.) This will induce even more defections to the Centrists, again leaving the Democrats and Republicans more radical than before. And so on, and so on, and so on. The likely equilibrium is a three-party system in which the Republicans and Democrats are left with their hard-core "base" while the Centrist Party comprises all the voters in between.

Second, a Centrist presence in the Senate is likely to encourage a few defections *among sitting senators*. If there were a bloc of four or five Centrists in the Senate in 2012, Olympia Snowe might have left the Republican Party to become a Centrist rather than quitting the Senate in disgust. Indiana's Richard Lugar might have run for reelection in Indiana as a Centrist rather than facing off against a Tea Party candidate in the Republican primary (which he ultimately lost)*. The Centrist Party is a logical home for incumbent senators exhausted by partisanship or facing electoral challenges from extremists in their own party.

Let's Make Things Better

This is not going to happen on its own. The Centrist Party has to be every bit as motivated as the Tea Party, albeit with a better intellectual focus. Everyday people—the same folks who lament the sad state of politics at a backyard barbecue—have to be excited by a better alternative. *And then we all have to do something about it.*

None of this will be easy. The same entrenched political operators who are steering our country in a ruinous direction will spend literally billions of dollars to protect their interests. The more formidable impediment is our

---

* The Tea Party challenger who beat Senator Lugar, State Treasurer Richard Mourdock, went on to lose the general election. This suggests that Lugar, who typically coasted to reelection in previous races, would have held his seat if he had not been knocked out of the race by the right flank of his own party.

own inertia. We all tend to be risk averse and unimaginative when it comes to change. There are a hundred reasons why a Centrist Party might fail, just as there are always reasons to be skeptical of any new business or art form or scientific discovery. I laughed out loud the first time someone explained to me the appeal of sending 140-character "tweets" to strangers. Of course, if I had invested in Twitter then, I would be much richer now.

The Centrist Party will work if we make it work. Never in the history of human civilization has it been easier to build a movement.

You can go to http://www.thecentristmovement.org and join the movement.

You can visit The Centrist Movement on Facebook at http://www.facebook.com/TheCentristMovement.

You can follow the Centrist Party on Twitter @Centristupdate.

The revolutionaries who believed that America should be independent from Britain had to print handbills, give speeches in taverns, and ride for days over muddy roads to mobilize their fellow citizens. We have the luxury of reaching millions of supporters in a fraction of the time it took George Washington to ride on horseback from Mt. Vernon to Philadelphia. There is no excuse for not trying to make things better.

If you think the American political system is broken, then you ought to do something about it. When your grandchildren ask you about the early-twenty-first century—about the growing debt and climate change and an increasingly dysfunctional Congress—are you going to explain how you sat in an armchair and complained a lot? Or are you going to be able to tell your grandchildren that you were a founding member of the Centrist Party?

IN THE WORDS of Victor Hugo, nothing is more powerful than an idea whose time has come.

The time for this idea has come. There is a better alternative to our broken system, and it can work. The Centrist ideology makes sense. The strategy does too. The American political system has reinvented itself in the past. We can do it again. We need an insurgency of the rational: a generation of Americans who are fed up with the current political system, who believe we can do better, and most important, who are ready to do something about it.

Are you one of those people?

Notes

1 *New York Times* exit polls for 2012 elections, http://elections .nytimes.com/2012/results/president/exit-polls (accessed January 2, 2013).

2 Thomas Friedman, "The Tea Kettle Movement," *New York Times*, September 29, 2010.

3 Organisation for Economic Co-operation, "OECD Health Data 2012—Frequently Requested Data," http://www.oecd.org/els/ healthpoliciesanddata/oecdhealthdata2012-frequentlyrequested data.htm (accessed January 2, 2013).

4 American Society of Civil Engineers, "Report Card for America's Infrastructure: 2009 Grades," http://www.infrastructurereport card.org/ (accessed January 2, 2013).

5 "Life in the Slow Lane," *Economist*, April 30, 2011.

6 Tamar Lewin, "Once a Leader, U.S. Now Lags in College Degrees," *New York Times*, July 23, 2010.

7 Charles M. Blow, "The G.O.P.'s Abandoned Babies," *New York Times*, February 26, 2011.

8 Peter G. Peterson Foundation, "The U.S. Spent More on Defense in 2011 Than Did the Countries with the Next 13 Highest Defense Budgets Combined," April 12, 2012, http://www.pgpf .org/Chart-Archive/0053_defense-comparison.aspx.

9 Yuichi Shoda, Walter Mischel, and Philip K. Peake, "Predicting Adolescent Cognitive and Self-Regulatory Competencies from Preschool Delay of Gratification: Identifying Diagnostic Conditions," *Developmental Psychology*, vol. 26, no. 6, 1990.

10 Mackenzie Weinger, "Poll: 73 Percent of Americans Say Country Headed in Wrong Direction," *Politico*, August 10, 2011, http://www.politico.com/news/stories/0811/61031.html.

11 "New Low: Just 14% Think Today's Children Will Be Better Off Than Their Parents," *Rasmussen Reports*, July 29, 2012, http://www.rasmussenreports.com/public_content/business/jobs_employment/july_2012/new_low_just_14_think_today_s_children_will_be_better_off_than_their_parents.

12 Matea Gold, "2012 Campaign Set to Cost a Record $6 Billion," *Los Angeles Times*, October 31, 2012.

13 Thomas Friedman, "Third Party Rising," *New York Times*, November 3, 2010.

14 David Brooks, "Pundit under Protest," *New York Times*, June 13, 2011.

15 Olympia Snowe, "Olympia Snowe: Why I'm Leaving the Senate," *Washington Post*, March 1, 2012.

16 Monica Davey, "Lugar Loses Primary Challenge in Indiana," *New York Times*, May 8, 2012.

17 Jennifer Steinhauer, "Weighing the Effect of an Exit of Centrists," *New York Times*, October 8, 2012.

18 Alan Murray, "A Raging Moderate Finds Neither Party Is Interested in Him," *Wall Street Journal*, March 2, 2004.

19 John P. Avlon, "What Independent Voters Want," *Wall Street Journal*, October 20, 2008.

20 David Brooks, "Party No. 3," *New York Times*, August 10, 2006.

21 "Congress Approval Ties All-Time Low at 10%," Gallup Politics, August 14, 2012, http://www.gallup.com/poll/156662/congress-approval-ties-time-low.aspx.

22 "Quigley Right Choice for 5th District Seat," *Chicago Sun-Times*, February 15, 2009.

23 "Price of Admission," Historical Elections, OpenSecrets.org, http://www.opensecrets.org/bigpicture/stats.php?display=A&type=A&cycle=2010 (accessed January 2, 2013).

24 David Brooks, "Thurston Howell Romney," *New York Times*, September 17, 2012.

25 Author was shadowing Paul Tsongas while reporting on his presidential campaign. The date of the exact quote is unknown, but it was during the fall of 1991.

26 "Rick Santorum's Ride," *Economist*, January 7, 2012.

27 "Carbon Taxes II," IGM Forum, Initiative on Global Markets, Chicago Booth, December 4, 2012, http://www.igmchicago.org/igm-economic-experts-panel/poll-results?SurveyID=SV_8oAB K2TolkGluV7.

28 USA Today/Gallup poll, August 4–7, 2011, "Americans Want New Debt Supercommittee to Compromise," Gallup Politics, August 10, 2011, http://www.gallup.com/poll/148919/ameri cans-new-debt-supercommittee-compromise.aspx.

29 Thomas E. Mann and Norman J. Ornstein, *It's Even Worse Than It Looks: How the American Constitutional System Collided with the New Politics of Extremism.* New York: Basic Books, 2012, p. xiv.

30 Gerald F. Seib, "The Politics of the Debt Ceiling," *Wall Street Journal*, April 26, 2011.

31 Amy Gutmann and Dennis F. Thompson, "How to Free Congress's Mind," *New York Times*, November 20, 2011.

32 USA Today/Gallup poll, August 4–7, 2011, "Americans Want New Debt Supercommittee to Compromise," Gallup Politics, August 10, 2011, http://www.gallup.com/poll/148919/americans-new-debt -supercommittee-compromise.aspx.

33 Chris Isidore and James O'Toole, "Hostess Brands Closing for Good," *CNNMoney*, November 16, 2012, http://money.cnn.com/2012/11/16/news/companies/hostess-closing/index.html.

34 Kenneth Sheve and Matthew Slaughter, "A New Deal for Globalization," *Foreign Affairs*, July/August 2007.

35 "World Health Organization Assesses the World's Health Systems," World Health Organization, June 21, 2000. Summary of findings from *The World Health Report 2000—Health Systems:*

Improving Performance, http://www.who.int/whr/2000/media_
centre/press_release/en/.

36 "For First Time, Majority of Americans Favor Legal Gay Marriage,"
    Gallup Politics, May 20, 2011, http://www.gallup.com/poll/147662/
    First-Time-Majority-Americans-Favor-Legal-Gay-Marriage.aspx.

37 "Plenty of Common Ground Found in Abortion Debate," Gallup
    Politics, August 8, 2011, http://www.gallup.com/poll/148880/
    Plenty-Common-Ground-Found-Abortion-Debate.aspx.

38 Gilda Sedgh et al., "Induced Abortion: Incidence and Trends
    Worldwide from 1995 to 2008," *Lancet,* vol. 379, no. 9816, Febru-
    ary 2012, pp. 625–632.

39 *National Vital Statistics Reports,* vol. 60, no. 3, December 29, 2011,
    table 18. Data are from 2009.